Alaska Warbird Survivors 2002

Warbird Survivors

Alaska Warbird Survivors 2002

A Handbook on where to find them

Harold A. Skaarup

Writers Club Press
San Jose New York Lincoln Shanghai

Alaska Warbird Survivors 2002
A Handbook on where to find them

All Rights Reserved © 2001 by Harold A. Skaarup

No part of this book may be reproduced or transmitted in any form or by any means, graphic, electronic, or mechanical, including photocopying, recording, taping, or by any information storage retrieval system, without the permission in writing from the publisher.

Writers Club Press
an imprint of iUniverse, Inc.

For information address:
iUniverse, Inc.
5220 S. 16th St., Suite 200
Lincoln, NE 68512
www.iuniverse.com

The aircraft described in Alaska Warbird Survivors and the locations listed for them may change from time to time. Although every effort has been made to ensure accuracy up to the time of publication, there are always amendments to be made. Updates to any of the information found in this handbook would be greatly appreciated, and every effort will be made to include them in future editions.

ISBN: 0-595-20918-1

Printed in the United States of America

Dedication

This book is dedicated to all the highly professional men and women of the American and Canadian Armed Forces of North American Aerospace Defence Command (NORAD). Many of them served in or worked with the military aircraft described in this handbook. Because of this service, you and I can sleep soundly at night. May it continue to be so.

EPIGRAPH

To control the air, aircraft bring certain characteristics which are not shared by land or sea forces—the ability to carry weapons over long ranges at great speed, the ability to concentrate rapidly large forces over a distant point, the ability to switch targets and to surprise and deceive—in a word, flexibility.[1]

[1.] John Pimlot, *Strategy & Tactics of Air Warfare*, Chartwell Books, Secaucus, New Jersey, 1979, p. 80.

Contents

List of Illustrations xi
Foreword xiii
Preface xv
Acknowledgements xvii
List of Abbreviations xix
Introduction xxv
1. Aircraft on display in Alaska 1
2. Alphabetical List of Military Aircraft Preserved in Alaska 13
3. Other Aircraft on display in Alaska 58
4. A Brief History of the Air War in the Pacific during WWII 64
5. Korean War Notes 88
6. Viet Nam Data 91
7. Post Viet Nam Military Buildup 95
8. The Gulf War 97
9. Continuing Service 108
10. Statement of the Secretary of Defense on the War on Terrorism 110
11. Japanese Aircraft that participated in attacks on Alaska 114
Appendix A—Short List of Alaska Warbird Survivors 117
Bibliography 123
About the Author 127

List of Illustrations

1. Lockheed E-3A Sentry AWACs, Yakula 27 Memorial xxi
2. Bell UH-1H Iroquois "Huey" (Serial No.) 14
3. Boeing B-29 Superfortress (Lady of the Lake) 15
4. Consolidated PBY-5A (wreck) (Serial No.) 21
5. Consolidated PBY-5A (NMNA) 21
6. Convair F-102A Delta Dagger (Serial No. 56-01274) 23
7. Curtiss P-40E Warhawk (wreck) (Serial No.) 24
8. Curtiss P-40 Warhawk (USAFM) 25
9. De Havilland DH-4 27
10. Douglas C-47A Skytrain (Serial No. 0315497) 29
11. Fairchild C-123J Provider (Serial No. 56-4395) 31
12. Fairchild A-10 Thunderbolt II (Serial No. 75-0289) 32
13. General Dynamics F-16A Fighting Falcon
    (Serial No. 78-0052) 33
14. Grumman J2F-6 Duck (Serial No.) (USAFM) 34
15. Lockheed P-38G Lightning (Serial No. 42-13400) 37
16. Lockheed P-80 Shooting Star (Serial No. 91849) 39
17. Lockheed T-33A Shooting Star (Serial No. 53-5403) 40
18. Martin B-10 Bomber (Serial No.) (USAFM) 41
19. McDonnell F-4C Phantom II
    (Serial No. 64-0890), painted as 66-723 44
20. McDonnell Douglas F-15 Eagle (Serial No. 74081) 46
21. North American T-6G Texan
    (Serial No. 453015A), painted as 34555 48

22. North American F-86A Sabre (Serial No. 12807) 50
23. Northrop F-89 Scorpion (Serial No. 32453) 52
24. Piasecki (Vertol) CH-21B Shawnee Helicopter 53
25. Sikorsky HO4S Helicopter (Serial No.) (USAFM) 54

Foreword

During the twentieth century, civil and military aviation has played a prominent role in the history and development of Alaska. Commercial operators have exploited the advantages offered by aircraft to overcome the unique challenges of geography and climate. By virtue of Alaska's strategic location on the continent's northwest flank looking out over the Pacific and facing Russia, a wide variety of military aircraft have been based there through the years.

The list of military aircraft types that made up the tapestry of Alaskan aviation is as extensive as the list of legendary figures who have contributed to its amazing history. While most of the military aircraft types no longer grace the airspace over Alaska, many can be viewed in their former splendor as they stand as gate guards or museum exhibits. This booklet provides a comprehensive guide to where these restored aircraft can be found. Complementing the details concerning aircraft specifications and roles, the author has included many facts. Finally, the descriptions of the recovery, restoration and preservation efforts stand as a tribute to the many volunteers who have devoted time, energy and financial support to ensure this rich heritage is preserved.

Paul A. Drover
Colonel
Deputy Commander
Alaskan NORAD Region
Elmendorf Air Force Base, Alaska

Preface

There are a number of us who have a continuing interest in retired military aircraft that are preserved in the state of Alaska. Many of these old warbirds can be found on the airfields at Elmendorf and Eielson Air Force Bases, as well as in the Alaska Aviation Heritage Museum in Anchorage, the Alaskaland Pioneer Air Museum in Fairbanks and as gate guardians at Kulis Air National Guard Base in Anchorage. Many other military aircraft are not on display, although their remains can be found in different crash sites scattered throughout the Alaskan bush.

Many examples of aircraft that saw service with the United States Army Air Corps (USAAF), the United States Army Air Force (USAF), the United States Navy (USN), and the United States Coast Guard (USCG) have been or are currently being salvaged and preserved, particularly where they are of significant historical interest. As an army officer and aviation enthusiast, historian, artist, and photographer, I am attempting to keep track of where a good number of these "warbird survivors" are presently located, and specifically for this book, where those aircraft can be found on display in Alaska.

The purpose of this handbook is to provide a simple checklist of where the surviving military aircraft in Alaska are now, and to provide at least one photograph of each type of aircraft mentioned. Former military aircraft are continuing to be being recovered from their crash sites, or traded or brought back from owners who have been flying them in other countries. In spite of this, there are still an incredible number of warbirds from American's aviation heritage for which no single example exists anywhere in the world, and many for which none exist in the USA. This handbook lists the warbird survivors that can be found in Alaska alphabetically by manufacturer, number and aircraft type. This list is also appended with a brief summary of the aircraft presently on display within the state by location, and a bit of the warbird's history in the US military. Due to space limitations, a selection of only those warbirds that can be found in Alaska is provided. If you are interested in other aviation books like this one, they can be found at the iUniverse.com on-line bookstore.

No list can ever be completely up to date, so if you as a reader have additional information to add, please forward an update to me at 2110 Cloverdale Drive, Colorado Springs, CO, 80920, or email me at *h.skaarup@worldnet.att.net*.

It is my sincere hope that the list of Alaska Warbird Survivors will continue to grow, as more of them are recovered and restored. Grant that you find the handbook useful. Cheers, Harold A. Skaarup

Acknowledgements

I would like to acknowledge each and every member of the museum staffs, particularly the volunteers in the aviation history sections in Anchorage, and at Elmendorf AFB, specifically John Cloe, and MSgt Joe Ord at Eielson AFB. Their patience and assistance has been invaluable in helping me to ensure that the data that has gone into the compilation of this handbook is as complete and accurate as it can be at the time of printing. Their support and assistance in tracking down the information pertaining to each of the individual aircraft listed here is greatly appreciated.

I would like to make special mention of the generous assistance provided by Deb Davis, who works at Elmendorf AFB, for her work in reviewing the AK WBS manuscript. Many thanks Deb.

List of Abbreviations

AFB	Air Force Base
AAHMK	Alaska Aviation Heritage Museum
AK	Alaska
AK ANG	Alaska Air National Guard
AFB	Air Force Base
ANG	Air National Guard
APAM	Alaskaland Pioneer Air Museum
CF	Canadian Forces
KANGB	Kulis Air National Guard Base
MAT&I	Museum of Alaska Transportation and Industry
NAS	Naval Air Station
NMNA	National Museum of Naval Aviation
NORAD	North American Aerospace Command
USAAF	United States Army Air Force
USAF	United States Air Force
USAFM	United States Air Force Museum
USCG	United States Coast Guard
USMC	United States Marine Corps
USN	United States Navy
USPACOM	United States Pacific Command
USSPACECOM	United States Space Command

YUKLA 27 MEMORIAL

On 22 September 1995, the United States Air Force and Canadian Forces lost 24 of their finest people with the catastrophic accident of an E-3 Airborne Warning and Control System (AWACS) aircraft. This aircraft was better known within the Elmendorf and Anchorage communities by its call sign, "Yukla 27". The aircraft crashed soon after takeoff from Elmendorf Air Force Base, Alaska. It was the first crash of a U.S. E-3. The

aircraft went down at about 7:45 a.m. in a heavily wooded area about two miles northeast of the runway. The AWACS was headed out on a seven-hour surveillance training mission.

An Air Force investigating officer from Headquarters Pacific Air Forces determined the crash resulted from the aircraft's two left-wing engines ingesting several Canada geese. According to the accident investigator, engine number two lost all power and engine number one experienced severe damage after ingesting the geese shortly after takeoff. The resulting loss of thrust rendered the Airborne Warning and Control System aircraft uncontrollable. After a slow, left climbing turn, the aircraft pitched downward and crashed. Human error on the part of the crew was not a factor.

The memorial, partially pictured above, was dedicated in September 1996 to honor the professionalism and dignity of the 24 crew members of Yukla 27 each of whom is remembered here.

Richard G. Leary, Lieutenant Colonel, USAF
Navigator
Richard P. Stewart II, Major, USAF
Mission Crew Commander
Marlon R. Thomas, Major, USAF
Mission Crew Commander
Steve Tuttle, Major, USAF
Airborne Surveillance Officer
Glenn "Skip" Rogers, Captain, USAF
Pilot
Robert John Long, Captain USAF
Senior Director
Bradley W. Paakola, Captain, USAF
Pilot
Carlos Alberto Arriaga, First Lieutenant, USAF
Weapons Director

Stephen C. O'Connel, Master Sergeant, USAF
Advanced Air Surveillance Technician
Bart L. Holmes, Technical Sergeant, USAF
Flight Engineer
Ernest R. Parrish, Technical Sergeant, USAF
Area Specialist
Dave Pitcher, Sergeant, CAF
Battle Director Technician
Charles D. Sweet, Jr., Technical Sergeant, USAF
Airborne Radar Technician
Brian K. Vanleer, Technical Sergeant, USAF
Advanced Air Surveillance Technician
Mark Alan Bramer, Technical Sergeant, USAF
Flight Engineer
Timothy B. Thomas, Technical Sergeant, USAF
Computer Display Maintenance Technician
Mark A. Collins, Technical Sergeant, USAF
Communications Systems Operator
J.P. Legault, Master Corporal, CAF
Communications Technician
Scott A. Bresson, Staff Sergeant, USAF
Airborne Radar Technician
Raymond O. Spencer, Jr., Staff Sergeant, USAF
Airborne Surveillance Technician
Joshua N. Weter, Senior Airman, USAF
Computer Display Maintenance Technician
Lawrence E. DeFrancesco, Senior Airman, USAF
Communications Systems Operator
Darien F. Watson, Airman, USAF
Airborne Surveillance Technician
Jeshua C. Smith, Airman, USAF
Airborne Surveillance Technician

INTRODUCTION

For those of you who are familiar with Alaska and its environs, the conditions can be harsh for an aviator. During my tour of duty with the Canadian Forces detachment based in Colorado Springs, I had the privilege of working at Elmendorf AFB with a good number of the highly professional men and women who serve NORAD there. The work had also given me the opportunity to examine a number of Alaska's warbird survivors close up, and to visit many of the sites where Alaska's aviation history has been made. These opportunities continue to be a privilege and an honour that are part of my military service, and I would therefore like to share some of the information I gathered with you. It is my hope that this book will show you where to find and view some of Alaska's veteran military aircraft, and to perhaps take an interest in some of the military aviation history which can be found in the arctic state. This book is specifically intended to provide a "where are they" guide for residents and visitors to Alaska who are interested in its rich resources of historical military aircraft.

I have had a serious interested in military aircraft for most of my life. My father served 20 years in the Royal Canadian Air Force (RCAF) and later the Canadian Forces (CF), and retired as a Warrant Officer in 1973. During his tour of duty, he also worked for NORAD while on station at Canadian Forces Base North Bay, Ontario.

As a Canadian Forces Army officer, the military has provided me with the opportunity to tour a number of aviation museums in North America and Europe. I was also lucky to have participated in a great number of airshows as both a civilian skydiver and military parachutist. These airshows gave me the opportunity to hear the sound of a P-51D Mustang and watch one tearing down a runway at full throttle (it still gets my blood pumping!). During these airshows, I never missed an opportunity to ask various owners of old WWII Warbirds such as the Mustang and Corsair, for permission to climb into the cockpit. Based on my flight experiences and observations to date, however, I concluded that you should never land in an airplane if you do not want to die in one. (I am equipped with "two perfectly serviceable parachutes" (that I pack myself), and you have only one airplane, and there is no such thing as a "perfectly serviceable airplane" as any mechanic will tell you).

I continue to serve as Army Intelligence officer with the Canadian Forces, and it is my great good fortune to have been posted to Colorado Springs, where I work for HQ NORAD and USSPACECOM up on the Cheyenne Mountain Air Force Station (CMAFS). During my tour of duty, I had the occasion to work at Elmendorf AFB and have visited a number of other locations and museums in Alaska. Although I am in the army, I've never lost my fascination for old warbirds. Because of this, I continue to identify and research the locations of as many of them as possible. I then attempt to verify their serial numbers through the United States Air Force Museum and the National Museum of Naval Aviation, and to photograph the aircraft, wherever they may be on display.

The main reason that I am producing this book is to provide other interested aviation enthusiasts with the kind of guide-book that I would liked to have had before arriving in Alaska to work with the servicemen and women who are part of NORAD and PACOM. This guide-book should tell the aircraft hunter where he or she may still find these warbirds and gate guardians, and, where possible, a way to contact the museums and airfields that display them for more information on the aircraft. If you have a further interest in this kind of information, there are other warbird survivor books in this series, which are available through Barnes and Noble as well as the iUniverse.com and Amazon.com online bookstores.

I believe that the volunteers who put so much time, effort and energy into maintaining and preserving the numerous retired military and historic aircraft found in Alaska deserve an enormous amount of praise and credit for their work. It is my hope that this handbook, "Alaska Warbird Survivors," provides the information and perhaps an incentive, that will bring you to visit their museums and to appreciate the rich resources of aviation heritage they are preserving on your behalf. The displays and exhibits are bound to change. Aircraft that have already been recovered from crash sites in Alaska include a P-40E, a P-38J, a B-26 and a B-24 which have gone to the Hill Museum in the lower 48 states. Hopefully, many more examples of USAF, USN, USMC and USA, and USANG aircraft will be added to the collections as they are retired, and equally important, perhaps many more will be recovered, refurbished and preserved in Alaska.

It will not be long before an update to this record is required. In the meantime, if you find that I've missed any aircraft that are presently on display in Alaska, or if there are bits and pieces of data you would like to see in the inevitable "revised and updated" version, please let me (and your museum staffs) know. My e-mail address is *h.skaarup@worldnet.att.net*. I sincerely hope that you find this handbook useful, and I look forward to seeing the appearance of more of Alaska's vanished warbirds as they are discovered, recovered, restored and put on display.

Blue skies, Harold A. Skaarup

AIRCRAFT ON DISPLAY IN ALASKA

Aircraft Museums and Military Gate Guardians in Alaska

The surviving USAAC, USAAF, USAF, USN, USMC, USCG and AK ANG warbirds on display in Alaska can be found in a great number of locations. The major aviation museums in the state as well as private displays of historical warbirds are listed here.

Atka Island

Atka Island, aircraft crash site
Consolidated B-24D Liberator (Serial No.), on the National Register

Eareckson Air Force Station

Eareckson AFS is located on Shemya Island, in the Bering Sea, 1,500 miles south-west of Anchorage in a small cluster of rocks known as the Near Islands. The Near Islands are near the international date line: Travel a few miles south on a Sunday and you will find yourself in Monday. Shemya's black volcanic sand inspired its traditional name, "Black Pearl of the Aleutians," but those who live there commonly call it "The Rock," for obvious reasons.

The U.S. military first came to Shemya in 1943 to build a runway to accommodate B-29 Superfortresses, but the largest bombers that ever flew from there during WWII were B-24 Liberators. Even today, you can still find many structures from those days, such as bunkers, 37mm anti-aircraft gun emplacements, and the remains of a gun in the courtyard of Building 600, where the barber and beauty shops are now located.

Today, Eareckson is operated by administrative contractors and the 611th Air Support Group.[2] For more information, call the Public Affairs Representatives at 907-392-3401, or John Cloe, the Historian at Elmendorf AFB, 907-552-5217.

There are no aircraft on display at Eareckson AFS, but there are a number of aircraft crash sites on islands nearby.

Anchorage, Kulis Air National Guard Base

The Alaska Air National Guard (AKANG) was organized in 1952 as the 8144th Air Base Squadron at Elmendorf AFB, operating T-6 aircraft with the Alaskan Air Command (AAC) as its gaining command. In 1955, it moved to Kulis ANG Base (adjacent to Anchorage International Airport) and was designated the 144th Fighter Bomber Squadron flying T-33, F-80 and F-86 aircraft. In 1957, airlift became its primary mission and the unit designation became the 144th Air Transport Squadron (ATS) Medium. In 1969, a parent organization was created and was designated the 176th Tactical Airlift Group (TAG).

[2.] Dan Cragg, *Guide to Military Installations, 4th Edition*, Stackpole Books, Mechanicsburg, PA, 1994, pp. 11-12.

The 176th's mission has remained "composite". In late 1987 it was announced that the 176th would assume the Air Force Search and Rescue mission in the Alaska Theater because the USAF's 71st Aerospace Rescue and Recovery Squadron at Elmendorf AFB was being deactivated.

The gaining command for the 176th and all of its subordinate units, except for the Aerial Port Flight and the 210 RQS, was changed to the Pacific Air Forces (PACAF) on 1 June 1992. 11AF, headquartered at Elmendorf AFB, became the unit's numbered Air Force. The flying units were concurrently redesignated the 144th Airlift Squadron (AS) and the 210th Rescue Squadron (RQS). The 210 RQS became PACAF-gained on 1 January 1993. At the same time, the Air National Guard reorganization was implemented and the 176th Composite Group was redesignated the 176th Group.

On 01 October 1995, the 176th Group was redesignated the 176th Wing. In early 1996, the 210 RQS received three new HC-130(H)N aircraft from the Lockheed Factory and transferred its two original C-130's to the New York ANG. In mid 1996, the 176th Aerial Port Flight was finally gained as a PACAF unit. Also in 1996, the Wing began conversion of the two flying squadrons to deployment tasking. At the close of 1996, the 176th Wing possesses 9 C-130H aircraft for the Airlift mission and 4 HC-130(H)N and 6 HH-60 aircraft for the Rescue mission.[3]

Kulis ANG Base Museum, 6000 Air Guard Road, Anchorage, 99502-1998. Tel: 907-249-1176.

[3.] http://www.fas.org/irp/agency/usaf/ang/alaska/176wg/

Brief descriptions of each type of aircraft on display in Alaska will be found at Annex A. The following aircraft are on display at Kulis ANG Base:

Douglas C-47A Skytrain (Serial No. 0315497)
Fairchild C-123J Provider (Serial No. 56-4395)
Lockheed P-80 Shooting Star (Serial No. 91849)
Lockheed T-33A Shooting Star (Serial No. 53-5403) (53-5096)
North American T-6G Texan (Serial No. 453015A), painted as 34555
North American F-86A Sabre (Serial No. 12807)

Eielson Air Force Base

Eielson was known simply as "Mile 26" when it opened in 1943, because it was the site of a U.S. Army Signal Corps telegraph station exactly 26 miles from Fairbanks that provided a link with Valdez, Alaska. It also sits 110 miles south of the Arctic Circle. During World War II, Eielson served as a storage area for excess Lend-Lease aircraft on their way to Russia, and Russian airmen were stationed there to take their possession. On 04 February 1948, Mile 26 was redesignated Eielson Air Force Base in honor of Carl Ben Eielson, a famed arctic pioneer and aviator. Today the base is home for the 343rd Wing, whose pilots fly the F-16 Fighting Falcon and the OA-10 Thunderbolt II. The wing's primary mission is to provide close-air support and forward air control for Army ground forces in Alaska. Approximately 3,000 active-duty personnel and their 4,300 dependents call Eielson home.[4]

For more information write to: 354th Wing Public Affairs Office, 3112 Broadway Ave., Ste. 5, Eielson AFB, AK, 99702-1870, or call 907-377-2116.

Brief descriptions of each type of aircraft on display will be found at Annex A. The following aircraft are on display at Eielson AFB:

[4.] Dan Cragg, *Guide to Military Installations, 4th Edition*, Stackpole Books, Mechanicsburg, PA, 1994, p. 13.

Cessna O-2A Skymaster (Serial No. 68-11003)
Fairchild A-10 Thunderbolt II (Serial No. 75-0289)
General Dynamics F-16A Fighting Falcon (Serial No. 78-0052)
McDonnell F-4C Phantom II (Serial No. 64-0905)
Lockheed T-33 Shooting Star (Serial No. 53-6064), under restoration

There are a number of aircraft crash sites near Eielson AFB, including the wreckage of two B-24 Liberators and the site of an O-38 which crashed in 1936 and was recovered in 1969. The O-38 is now in the USAF Museum at Dayton, Ohio.

Elmendorf Air Force Base

Elmendorf Air Force Base lies farther north than Helsinki, Finland, and is almost as far west as Hawaii, but it lies on the northern suburbs of Alaska's largest city, some 1,400 air miles from Seattle. With a population over 235,000, Anchorage has almost 50% of the total population of the state of Alaska.

Elmendorf began as an airfield called Fort Richardson. In November 1940 the field was designated Elmendorf Field, after Hugh M. Elmendorf. In March 1951, the Army relocated its garrison to the new Fort Richardson, on the southeast side of Anchorage, and the installation came under the authority of the Air Force. Today the base's 13,000-square-acre expanse is home for the 3rd Wing Group, HQ 21st TFW/FA, whose pilots fly two squadrons the F-15C/D Eagle, and one squadron each of F-15E Strike Eagles, E-3A AWACs, and C-130s/C-12 transports. Approximately 7,000 active-duty personnel and 10,900 dependents and 2,400 civilian employees call Elmendorf home.[5]

---

5. Ibid, p. 14.

For more information write to Public Affairs Office, 3rd Wing, Elmendorf AFB, AK, 99506-2530, or call 907-552-1110.

Brief descriptions of each type of aircraft on display will be found at Annex A. The following aircraft are on display at Elmendorf AFB:

Convair F-102A Delta Dagger (Serial No.56-01274)
Lockheed P-38G Lightning (Serial No. 42-13400)
Lockheed T-33A Shooting Star (Serial No. 53-6021)
McDonnell F-4C Phantom II (Serial No. 66-723)
McDonnell F-4C Phantom II (Serial No. 66-0890)
McDonnell Douglas F-15A Eagle (Serial No. 94081)
Northrop F-89J Scorpion (Serial No. 32453)
Piasecki CH-21 Shawnee helicopter (Serial No. 52-8696), painted as 0-28696

Anchorage, Alaska Aviation Heritage Museum

Anchorage, Alaska Aviation Heritage Museum, 4721 Aircraft Drive, Lake Hood, 99502. Tel: 800-770-5325, or 907-248-5325.

The *AAHM* holds 25 rare historical aircraft, most of which are bushplanes but a number of which are military aircraft as well. In addition to the aircraft, the museum has a display that includes dozens of rare photographs and memorabilia exhibits gathered from famous pioneers and veterans. The museum is located on the south side of the Lake Hood Seaplane Base-Anchorage International Airport. The museum is open 7 days a week from 10 AM to 6 PM 15 may through to 15 September.

Brief descriptions of each type of aircraft on display will be found at Annex A. The following aircraft are on display at the *AAHM*:

American Pilgrim 100B (Serial No.)
Beechcraft UC-45F Expeditor (Serial No.)
Bell UH-1H Iroquois "Huey" (Serial No.)
Bellanca Pacemaker CH-300 (Serial No.)
Bellanca Sr. Pacemaker (fuselage) (Serial No.)
Cessna T-50 Bushmaster (Serial No.)
Consolidated PBY-5A Catalina Canso (wreck) (Serial No.)
Curtiss Robin (Serial No.)
Douglas DWC World Cruiser "Seattle" (Serial No.)
Fairchild 24G (Serial No.)
Fairchild FC2W2 (frame) (Serial No.)
Ford 5-AT Trimotor (1929 wreckage) (Serial No.)
Grumman Goose G-21A (Serial No.)
Grumman G-44 Widgeon (Serial No.)
Grumman J2F-6 Duck (Serial No.)
Hamilton Metalplane H47 (Serial No.)
Keystone Loening K1-84 (Serial No.)
Noordyn C-64A Norseman Mk. IV (Serial No.)
S-43 (nose only) (Serial No.)
Spartan Executive (Serial No.)
Spencer Aircar (Serial No.)
Stearman C2B (Serial No.)
Stinson AT-19 Reliant (Serial No.)
Stinson L-5 Sentinel (Serial No.)
Stinson SR Jr.(Serial No.)
Stinson SR-9 Gullwing CM (Serial No.)
Stinson 108 (Serial No.)
Travel Air 6000B (float) (Serial No.)
Waco UIC (Serial No.)
Waco YKC (float) (Serial No.)

Fairbanks, Alaskaland Pioneer Air Museum

Fairbanks, Alaskaland Pioneer Air Museum, 2300 Airport Way, 99701. Tel: 907-451-0037 or 452-2969. Mail POB 70437, 99707-0437. *http://www.akpub.com/akttt/aviat.html.*

The museum began in 1982 when a local group had a dream to preserve the early aviation history of Alaska that began in Fairbanks. The first airplane was in the Interior of Alaska in 1913, and the first commercial flight began in 1923.

Alaska is a huge state, and weather conditions and equipment needed to fly the Interior and Arctic Alaska are different from the coastal area, therefore, the reason for the parent name.

The Alaskaland Centennial Park offered an unoccupied building to the IAAAF thus the Alaskaland Pioneer Air Museum was born. The building, a large tetrahedron structure, 134 feet in diameter and 38 feet high, and known as the Gold Dome, is located in the center of Alaskaland. The Air Museum was opened in 1992. (APAM)

The museum is open from Memorial Day to Labor Day, 11 AM to 9 PM.

Brief descriptions of each type of aircraft on display will be found at Annex A. The following aircraft are on display at the *APAM*:

Baking Duce II (F.M. 1) (Serial No.)
Beech UC-45F (Serial No.)
Bell UH-1H Iroquois "Huey" helicopter (Serial No.)
Fairchild 24J (Serial No.)
Fokker Super Universal (frame) (Serial No.)
Martyn B-10 Bomber (Serial No.)
MX Quicksilver (Serial No.)

Noordyn C-64A Norseman Mk. IV (Serial No.)
Pereira S.P. 3 (Serial No.)
Raven S-50 (Serial No.)
Rotorway 133 (Serial No.)
Rutan Vari-EZ (Serial No.)
Ryan PT-22 (ST3KR) (Serial No.)
Sikorsky HO4S Chickasaw helicopter
Stinson SR-5 Jr. (Serial No.)
Vultee V-77/AT-19 Reliant (Serial No.)

Healy, Denali Wings

Healy, Denali Wings, Box 254, Healy, Alaska, 99743, Tel: 907-683-2245.

Brief descriptions of each type of aircraft on display will be found at Annex A. The following aircraft is on display at Healy:
Ford Tri-Motor (Serial No.)

Kenai

Kenai, City static display
Lockheed T-33A Shooting Star (Serial No. 52-9772)

Wasilla, Museum of Alaska Transportation and Industry

Wasilla, Museum of Alaska Transportation & Industry, 3800 Neuser Drive, Wasilla, Alaska, 99687. PO Box 909, 99645. Tel: 907-376-1211, or 907-745-4493.

Brief descriptions of each type of aircraft on display will be found at Annex A. The following aircraft are on display at Wasilla.

Bell UH-1H Iroquois "Huey" (Serial No.)
Bowers 1-A Flybaby (homebuilt)
Cessna T-50 Bobcat (Serial No.)
Convair F-102A Delta Dagger (Serial No. 56-01282)
Cunningham-Hall PT-6 (1929)
Douglas C-47 Skytrain (Serial No.)
Douglas C-47A Skytrain (Serial No.)
Fairchild 71 (1929)
Fairchild C-123J Provider (Serial No.)
Fike "E" (homebuilt)
German V-1 "Buzz Bomb" replica, manufactured by Ford Motor Co. for testing)
Lockheed Electra 10A (Serial No.)
Mitchell B-10 Flying Wing (ultra-light)
Piasecki H-21C Shawnee helicopter (Serial No. 52-4362)
Rotec Panther (ultra-light)
Sikorsky H-5H Dragonfly helicopter (Serial No. 49-02001) (9200)

Fort Greely

Located about 107 miles southeast of Fairbanks, Fort Greely covers some 650,000 acres and has been the site for the testing of a wide variety of military items since the Cold Regions Test Center was established there in 1949.

Named after Major-General Adolphus Washington Greely, arctic explorer, Fort Greely was established in June 1942 under the Lend-Lease program as a transfer point for American and Russian pilots. In August 1955, the post was designated Fort Greely. It is a small post in terms of population, with approximately 450 military personnel and their 300 dependents, and 700 civilian employees.[6]

There are no aircraft on display at Fort Greely.

Fort Richardson

Fort Richardson is close to the port city of Anchorage, and occupies 62,000 acres situated on the northeast side of the city adjacent to Elmendorf AFB. Rimming the city to the east are the Chugach Mountains.

The fort was named in honor of Brigadier-General Wilds P. Richardson, a pioneer explorer in Alaska. Fort Richardson was originally located on the site of Elmendorf AFB from 1940 to 1941 and moved to its present location in 1950. The post is home to the U.S. Army Garrison, Alaska, headquarters and to elements of the 6th Infantry Division (light), which has forces at both Fort Richardson and Fort Wainwright. The post supports a population of approximately 4,400 military personnel, 5,600 family members and 1,540 civilian employees.[7]

For more information write to: Public Affairs Office, 6th Infantry Division (Light), Attention: APVR-PR-PO, Fort Richardson, AK, 99505-5900, or call 907-384-2113/2072.

Fort Wainwright

Fort Wainwright is located just to the east of Fairbanks along the Chena River, some 350 miles by road north of Anchorage and 1,500 miles northwest of Dawson Creek, British Columbia, Canada, along the Alaska Highway. The fort is named after General Jonathan M. Wainwright, defender of Bataan against the Japanese in the Philippines during WWII.

[6.] Ibid, p. 15.
[7.] Ibid, p. 16.

The post began its existence in January 1961, when Ladd Air Force Base was transferred to the Army and renamed Fort Wainwright.[8]

For more information write to: Public Affairs Office, Fort Wainwright, AK, 99703-500, or call 907-353-6701.

Adak Naval Air Station

The U.S. Navy established a Naval Operating Base on Adak Island in 1942, and until it was deactivated, it was the site of several command and tenant activities, including the Adak Search and Rescue Coordination and Naval Security Group Activity.[9]

Aircraft on display in Alaska

The following is an alphabetical list of military aircraft on display in the State of Alaska. Where there are known survivors, a list of the museum or town site where they can be found is also included.

Each aircraft is identified as follows:

Aircraft Manufacturer, **Type**, **Code Name**, and the **Number** of this type of aircraft. A paragraph or narrative on each of the types identified is included and followed by location information as follows:

[Location of Survivors, (Mk., Serial Number, Colour Scheme), Notes].

---

[8] Ibid, p. 17.
[9] Ibid, p. 18, and Deb Davis, Elmendorf AFB.

Alphabetical List of Military Aircraft Preserved in Alaska

Beechcraft Model 18 Expeditor (UC45F) (N1047B)

The Beech Model 18 is a twin-engine light transport powered by a pair of 450-hp Pratt & Whitney R-985-AN-14B radial piston engines. The aircraft had a maximum speed of 220 mph, a service ceiling of 21,400', and a range of 1,530 miles. *The Complete Encyclopedia of World Aircraft.*

One of the most famous twin engine aircraft ever built, the Beech was used during WWII for communications work and instrument flying training. After the war, the Expeditor was used as a basic multi-engine trainer. First flown in 1937, the aircraft was used to train pilots and radio officers, transport VIPs, and as a general transport aircraft. Later in its career, the aircraft was often used in search and rescue (SAR) missions. The C-45 was the WW II military version of the popular Beechcraft Model 18 commercial light transport. Beech built a total of 4,526 of these aircraft for the Army Air Forces between 1939 and 1945 in four versions, the AT-7 Navigator navigation trainer, the AT-11 Kansan bombing-gunnery trainer, the C-45 Expeditor utility transport and the F-2 for aerial photography and mapping. The AT-7 and AT-11 versions were well-known to WW II navigators and bombardiers, for most of these men received their training in these aircraft. Thousands of AAF pilot cadets also were given advanced training in twin-engine Beech airplanes. *Information courtesy of the US Air Force Museum.*

Alaska UC45Fs were used for search and rescue by the Army Air Forces. After the war, N1047B was operated by Ward Air Service in Juneau. *AAHM.*

Bell 205 UH-1H Iroquois "Huey" Helicopter (Serial No.) *(HAS Photo)*

The Bell UH-1H is a general-purpose utility helicopter powered by one 1,400-hp Avco Lycoming T5313B turboshaft. This helicopter had a maximum speed of 127 mph, a service ceiling of 12,600' and a range of 318 miles. *The Complete Encyclopedia of World Aircraft.*

The HU-1 evolved from a 1955 Army competition for a new utility helicopter. The Army employed it in various roles, later including that of an armed escort or attack gunship in Vietnam. The USAF, USN, and USMC eventually adopted the model as did Canada, Brazil, and West Germany. The initial Army designation was HU-1, which led to the common unofficial nickname of Huey. It was redesignated in 1962 as the UH-1 under a tri-service agreement. USAF orders for the Huey began in 1963 for UH-1Fs, intended for support duties at missile sites, and for TH-1Fs for instrument and hoist training and medical evacuation. The HH-1 H incorporated a longer fuselage and larger cabin for a crew of two and up to eleven passengers or six litters. The USAF ordered these in 1970 as local base rescue helicopters to replace the HH-43 Huskie. The first of the USAF's UH-1Ns, a twin-engine utility version capable of cruising on one engine, was obtained in 1970. *Information courtesy of the US Air Force Museum.*

There are two on display in Alaska, one with the Alaska Aviation Heritage Museum and another with the Alaskaland Pioneer Air Museum. The UH-1H on display with the *AAHM* served in Viet Nam before coming to Alaska with the U.S. Army. It was used for roughly 23 years for search and rescue efforts in Alaska before being flown in and donated to the museum. *AAHM.*

Boeing KB-29P Superfortress (Photo by Staff Sgt. Andrew N. Dunaway)

The Superfortress was a long-range strategic bomber and reconnaissance aircraft. The B-29 was introduced in June 1944, and at the time represented a tremendous leap forward in technology. With four powerful 3,500-hp Pratt & Whitney R-4360-35 Wasp Major or four Wright R-3350-23-23A/-41 Cyclone 18 turbo-charged radial piston engines, it had the speed of many fighters (358 mph). The aircraft had a service ceiling of 31,850' and a range of 3,250 miles. The B-29 was heavily armed with two .50 cal machine-guns in each of four remotely-controlled power-operated gun turrets and three .50 cal machine-guns and one 20mm cannon in the tail turret. It could carry a bomb-load of 20,000 lbs. *The Complete Encyclopedia of World Aircraft.*

The B-29 was the largest and most sophisticated bomber to enter combat in WWII. First flown in 1942 with initial production models revealed in 1943. Although plagued by engine problems early on it was an extremely strong, stable and efficient ac. A favorite with crews, due to pressurized and heated crew compartments. It had sophisticated RADAR and defensive armament. It served well in the Pacific during WWII, in Korea and then in the Strategic Air Command. Several versions were produced including an aerial re-fueling tanker. It was used as a launch platform for experimental super sonic aircraft. A total of 3979 aircraft were built.

The Superfortress primarily operated in the Pacific battle area, where it played a central role in the strategic campaign against Japan, which culminated in the dropping of Atomic bombs on Hiroshima (by the B-29 Enola Gay) and Nagasaki (by the B-29 Bocks Car). The Boeing B-29 was designed in 1940 as an eventual replacement for the B-17 and B-24. The first one built made its maiden flight on 21 September 1942. In December 1943 it was decided not to use the B-29 in the European Theater, thereby permitting the airplane to be sent to the Pacific area where its great range made it particularly suited for the long over-water flight required to attack the Japanese homeland from bases in China. During the last two months of 1944, B-29s began operating against Japan from the islands of Saipan, Guam and Tinian. With the advent of the conflict in Korea in June 1950, the B-29 was once again thrust into battle. For the next several years it was effectively used for attacking targets in North Korea. *Information courtesy of the US Air Force Museum.*

The "**Lady in the Lake**" at Eielson AFB is a KB-29P, the refueling version of the four-engine B-29 heavy bomber, Tail No. 4483905. She was powered by four 3,500-hp Pratt & Whitney R-4360-35 Wasp Major turbo-charged radial piston engines, and had a maximum speed of 385 mph, a service ceiling of 37,000', and a range of 4,650 miles. Her permanent home was Malmstrom Air Force Base, Mont., but she was on temporary duty at Eielson. She died April 17, 1956, according to records, when she landed on Eielson's runway and her front landing gear buckled. She stopped thanks to a snowbank. Her crew, who was practicing touch-and-go landings, was unharmed and she only suffered minor injuries. She might have survived had tow crews not fatally damaged her superstructure attempting to remove her from the snowbank and haul her across the hard runway.

In 1979, Ivan D. Smith, her co-pilot that fateful day, visited Eielson and recalled the crash during an interview.

"There wasn't any snow on the ground," said Smith. "If it had not been for the snowbanks along the runway, we'd have gone zipping off through the tulles on our merry way. Two of the props were a little dinged up, but most of the damage was done during the towing operations."

After an inspection, the decision was made to strip her of usable parts for salvage, according to a base fact sheet, because her replacement, KC-97 aerial tankers were already being phased into the Air Force inventory. (KC-97s were modified four-engine Boeing Model 367 versions of the Stratocruiser, designated the Stratotanker).

Stripped of her vital organs, No. 4483905 sat idle near the flightline for many years. She was finally hauled to a gravel pit off Transmitter Site Road during a base cleanup in the early '60s. As time passed, a lake formed around her and she was dubbed "Lady in the Lake."

Today, the top half of her cockpit, right wing and tail are the only parts normally visible above water. Besides woodland creatures and waterfowl, her company includes curious first-time visitors or base residents seeking a quiet place to think or read. Some visitors have braved the chilly water to place unit emblem stickers on her rusty remains.

The "Lady in the Lake" gave her best days to her country and its people, and continues resting silently and peacefully in her watery grave, serving as a reminder of past. (*Article by Tech. Sgt. Tammy Cournoyer, Air Force News Service, Released: May 29, 1998*).

Boeing Model 707 E-3A Sentry (AWACS)

The E-3A is an airborne early-warning and command post aircraft powered by four 21,000-lb thrust Pratt & Whitney TF33-PW-100/100A turbofan engines. It has a maximum speed of 530 mph, a service ceiling of 29,000', and a rate of endurance from home base of 6 hours. The aircraft is unarmed, but acts essentially as a flexible, jamming-resistant, mobile and survivable radar station, as well as a command, communications and control center, based on the well-proven B-707 airframe. The AWACS aircraft can provide all-weather identification and tracking over a variety of terrain, conducting aircraft interception and interdiction control, as well as working in a variety of reconnaissance roles. The most obvious feature of the aircraft is its large rotodome assembly mounted on two wide-chord stream-lined struts which are secured to the upper rear fuselage. Other elements of the system are carried within the Sentry's wings, fuselage, fin and tailplane. More powerful engines are used than in the original airliner version. 34 of these aircraft are in operation with the USAF, another 18 serve with NATO. E-3As are also in service with the governments of France, Saudi Arabia and the United Kingdom. A model of the E-3A is displayed with the Yukla Memorial at Elmendorf AFB. *Information courtesy of the US Air Force.*

Cessna T-50 Bushmaster

The Bushmaster is a five-seat light transport powered by two 245-hp Jacobs R-755-9 radial piston engines. The aircraft had a maximum speed of 195 mph, a service ceiling of 22,000', and a range of 750 miles. *The Complete Encyclopedia of World Aircraft.*

War-time expansion of Navy ferry squadrons and aircraft delivery units brought a need for small reliable transports to carry ferry pilots to and from their home bases at the end of delivery flights during World War II. Typical of the commercial types acquired by the Navy in 1942-43 to fill this need was the four/five seat Cessna T-50 bearing the Navy designation JRC-1 and affectionately called the Bamboo Bomber by those who flew it.

The aircraft was also acquired by the Army Air Forces under the designations of ATB and AT-17 and was used as a transition trainer for pilots who were going on to fly multi-engine type aircraft. *Information courtesy of the National Museum of Naval Aviation.*

Designed in the late 30's, the Cessna "Bobcat" was flown by the military for flight training. After WWII was over, many were surplused to civilian air carriers. Known as the "Bamboo Bomber" because of their all wood wing, many were used in Alaska air operations. Six examples were modified for bush operations by Ray Petersen's Northern Consolidated Airlines. Petersen called his modified Cessna T-50's "Bushmasters." The air museum's example, NC30023, was recovered from an aircraft dump in Nome in 1988. The wood wing of NC30023 was a 3-year restoration project by Walt Eberhart, a Fairbanks resident and a former NCA mechanic, who worked on NC30023 while the Cessna was in service with NCA. *AAHM*

Cessna O-2 Skymaster

The O-2 is a military version of the six-seat Cessna Model 337 Super Skymaster. Distinguished by twin tail booms and tandem-mounted engines, it features a tractor-pusher propeller arrangement. Derived from the Cessna Model 336, the Model 337 went into production for the civilian market in 1965. It is powered by two 210-hp Continental IO-360-GB flat-six piston engines, has a maximum speed of 206 mph, a service ceiling of 18,000', and a range of 1,422 miles. *The Complete Encyclopedia of World Aircraft.*

In late 1966, the USAF selected a military variant, designated the O-2, to supplement the O-1 Bird Dog forward air controller (FAC) aircraft then operating in Southeast Asia. Having twin engines enabled the O-2 to absorb more ground fire and still return safely, endearing it to its crews. The O-2 first flew in Jan. 1967 and production deliveries began in March. Production ended in June 1970 after 532 O-2s had been built for the USAF. The O-2A was extensively used in Vietnam, and a number served in Alaska.

Two series were produced: the O-2A and the O-2B. The O-2A is equipped with wing pylons to carry rockets, flares, and other light ordnance. In the FAC role the O-2A was used for identifying and marking enemy targets with smoke rockets, coordinating air strikes and reporting target damage. The O-2B was a psychological warfare aircraft equipped with loudspeakers and leaflet dispensers. It carried no ordnance. *Information courtesy of the US Air Force Museum.*

A Cessna O-2A Skymaster (Serial No. 68-11003) is on display at Eielson AFB.

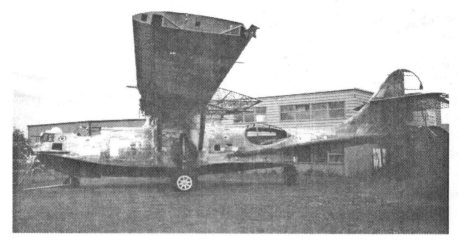

Consolidated PBY-5A Catalina/Canso (AAHM)) *(HAS Photo)*

Consolidated PBY-5A Catalina/Canso *(Photo courtesy of the National Museum of Naval Aviation)*

The PBY-5A is a seven or nine-seat long-range maritime patrol-bomber amphibian/flying boat, powered by two 1,200-hp Pratt & Whitney R-1830-92 Twin Wasp radial piston engines. The aircraft had a maximum speed of 179 mph, a service ceiling of 14,700', and a maximum range of 2,545 miles. *The Complete Encyclopedia of World Aircraft.*

The Catalina version of the PBY series seaplanes and amphibians was flown extensively by the Navy during WW II. It is a twin-engine, parasol-mounted monoplane equipped with a flying boat hull, retractable tricycle landing gear and retractable wing-tip floats. These used primarily for air-sea rescue work (DUMBO missions) with the AAF's Emergency Rescue Squadrons throughout WW II and for several years thereafter. During the war, OA-10 crews rescued hundreds of downed fliers.

The prototype Catalina first flew on March 28, 1935. It was produced by Consolidated Aircraft Corp. in both seaplane and amphibian versions. Catalinas were also produced by Canadian Vickers, Ltd. and the Naval Aircraft Factory. Eventually, nearly 2,500 Catalina derivatives were built for the Navy. Approximately 380 were transferred to the AAF as OA-10s, OA-10As, OA-10Bs or, in some cases, with their original Navy designations. Catalinas also were flown by a number of allied nations during and after WW II. *Information courtesy of the US Air Force Museum.*

The PBY-5A on display at the Alaska Aviation Heritage Museum (*AAHM*) was built in 1943, and is a wreck that was brought to the museum by Tarhe helicopter from its crash site at Dago Lake on the Alaska Peninsula. While operating with the 10th Rescue Squadron at Elmendorf AFB in 1947, the *AAHM* Catalina carried out an emergency landing caused by engine failure, at Dago Lake. The government declared the aircraft surplus, and it was purchased by the Richard's family, stripped of parts, and left at Dago Lake until 1984. A gigantic recovery project was conducted by the National Guard and air museum volunteers to finally bring the huge amphibian to the museum utilizing two Alaska helicopter operations in 1984 and 1987. *AAHM.*

Convair F-102A Delta Dagger *(HAS Photo)*

The Delta Dagger is a single-seat supersonic all-weather interceptor that is powered by one 17,200-lb after-burning thrust Pratt & Whitney J57-P-23 or –25 turbojet. It had a maximum speed of 825 mph, a service ceiling of 36,000', and a range of 1,350 miles. It was armed with two AIM-26 or 26A Falcon missiles, or one Falcon and two AIM-4C/D missiles in a weapons bay. *The Complete Encyclopedia of World Aircraft.*

The primary mission of the F-102 was to intercept and destroy enemy aircraft. It was the world's first supersonic all-weather jet interceptor and the USAF's first operational delta-wing aircraft. The F-102 made its initial flight on 24 October 1953 and became operational with the Air Defense Command in 1956. At the peak of deployment in the late 1950's, F-102s equipped more than 25 ADC squadrons. Convair built 1,101 F-102s, 975 of which were F-102As. The USAF also bought 111 TF-102s as combat trainers with side-by-side seating. In a wartime situation, after electronic equipment on board the F-102 had located the enemy aircraft, the F-102's radar would guide it into position for attack. At the proper moment, the electronic fire control system would automatically fire the F-102's air-to-air rockets and missiles. *Information courtesy of the US Air Force Museum.*

Delta Daggers served in the Pacific Air Forces from 1959 to 1970, where they were deployed to Thailand and South Vietnam during the conflict in South East Asia, and also with the Alaska Air National Guard from 1961 to 1976. There are two of these aircraft on display in Alaska, one at Elmendorf AFB and another at Wasilla, in the Museum of Alaska Transportation & Industry.

F-102A Serial No. 56-01274 on display at Elmendorf AFB is painted in the markings of the 317th Fighter Interceptor Squadron, which served as the only fighter interceptor squadron in Alaska from 1957 to 1969. F-102A Serial No. 56-01282 is on display at the Museum of Alaska Transportation and Industry in Wasilla.

Curtiss P-40 Warhawk (AAHM) *(HAS Photo)*

Curtiss P-40 Warhawk *(Photo courtesy of the US Air Force Museum)*

The Warhawk was the most numerous single-seat fighter-bomber in the US when the US entered WWII in December 1941. The Warhawk was powered by one 1,200-hp Allison V-1710-81 inline piston engine, and had a maximum speed of 343 mph, a service ceiling of 31,000', and a range of 1,080 miles. The armament varied, but the N version carried six wing-mounted .50 cal machine-guns and the aircraft could carry up to 1,500-lb of bombs. *The Complete Encyclopedia of World Aircraft.*

The P-40 had been developed from the P-36 Hawk, and was a durable aircraft that could take a lot of punishment and shoot back with a solid firepower. The nose design made the P-40 particularly suitable for the painting of shark's and dragon's teeth to give it the killer look in the air.

P-40s engaged Japanese aircraft during the attack on Pearl Harbor and the invasion of the Philippines in December 1941. They also were flown in China early in 1942 by the famed Flying Tigers and in North Africa in

1943 by the first AAF all-black unit, the 99th Fighter Squadron. The P-40 served in numerous combat areas, including the Aleutian Islands, Italy, the Middle East, the Far East, the Southwest Pacific and some were sent to Russia. Though often outclassed by its adversaries in speed, maneuverability and rate of climb, the P-40 earned a reputation in battle for extreme ruggedness. At the end of the P-40's brilliant career, more than 14,000 had been produced for service in the air forces of 28 nations. *Information courtesy of the US Air Force Museum.*

The P-40 Warhawk wreckage on display at the Alaska Aviation Heritage Museum was recovered from its WWII crash site in the interior and brought to Anchorage by helicopter on 16 September 1998. This Curtiss P-40E Warhawk was recovered from Unalaska Island in the Aleutians. It had crashed there after its pilot had been shot down on the evening of 4 June 1942, on the second day of the Battle of Dutch Harbor. The fighter was being flown at the time by Lt. Winfield E. McIntyre. He and other pilots from the 343rd Fighter Group based at Fort Glen Airfield on Umnak Island, had engaged a number of Japanese Zero fighters and Val dive bombers returning to their carriers after the attack on the US Navy Installation at Dutch Harbor. During the ensuing dogfight, McIntyre's P-40 was jumped by a Zero and set on fire. While trying to get the fire out, McIntyre put the aircraft into a steep dive. He then managed to carry out a wheels down landing on the island's rough terrain, but in then dug a wingtip into the ground which caused the aircraft to flip over onto its back.

McIntyre survived the shoot-down with relatively minor injuries and walked to a nearby beach. Here he was observed by the crew of a PBY Catalina (similar to the one on display with the AAHM), and they in turn sent a boat to pick him up. The P-40 remained in its inverted position until lifted out to the AAHM by a US Coast Guard Jayhawk helicopter, based on Kodiak. *(AAHM)*

De Havilland DH-4A *(HAS Photo)*

The DH-4A was an American-built two-seat day bomber variant of the British DH-4. The aircraft was powered by one 375-hp Rolls-Royce Eagle VIII inline piston engine, with a maximum speed of 143 mph, a service ceiling of 22,000', and an endurance of 3 hrs and 45 min. The DH-4A was an ever-present element of the US Army Air Service both during and following World War I. When the US entered World War I in April 1917, the Aviation Section of the Signal Corps only had 132 aircraft, all obsolete. Modeled from a combat tested British De Havilland design, the DH-4 was the only US built aircraft to see combat during World War I. During the war, the Air Service used the DH-4 primarily for day bombing, observation, and artillery spotting. The first American-built DH-4 arrived in France in May 1918, and the 135th Aero Squadron flew the first DH-4 combat mission in early August. 1,213 DH-4s were delivered to France by war's end.

With few funds to buy new aircraft in the years following World War I, the US Army Air Service used the DH-4 in a variety of roles, such as transport, air ambulance, photographic plane, trainer, target tug, forest fire patroller and even as an air racer. In addition, the US Post Office operated the DH-4 as a mail carrier.

The DH-4 also served as a flying test bed at McCook Field in the 1920s, testing turbo-superchargers, propellers, landing lights, engines, radiators, and armament. There were a number of notable DH-4 flights such as the astounding New York to Nome, Alaska flight in 1920, the record breaking transcontinental flight in 1922 by Jimmy Doolittle and the first successful air-to-air refueling in 1923.

1,538 DH-4s were modified in 1919-1923 to DH-4Bs by moving the pilot's seat back and the now unpressurized gas tank forward, correcting the most serious problems in the DH-4 design. A further improved version was the DH-4M whereby over 300 DH-4s received new steel tube fuselages. By the time it was finally retired from service in 1932, the DH-4 had developed into over 60 variants. *Information courtesy of the US Air Force Museum.* A model of the DH-4 is on display as shown above, near the P-38 exhibit at Elmendorf AFB.

Douglas World Cruiser "Seattle"

The DWC was a long-range experimental aircraft built in the year 1925. It had a two-man crew, and was powered by a single 420hp Liberty engine. It had a maximum speed of 102 mph, a service ceiling of 9,000' and a range of 2500 miles. It was a development of the DT-2 torpedo aircraft.

The Douglas DWC World Cruiser did exactly what its name indicated. Two out of four completed a 175-day, 44,800-km flight. This aircraft of the US Army Air Service was one of four biplanes that attempted the first flight in history to circumnavigate the globe. Two of the original four aircraft completed the trip. The "Seattle" crashed near Port Moller on the Alaska Peninsula and the wreckage was retrieved in 1967 through the efforts of Bob Reeve to go on display in the *Centennial Aviation Museum* that burned in 1973. The "Seattle" wreckage survived the fire and is now displayed at the Alaska Aviation Heritage Museum courtesy of the Alaska State Museum in Juneau. *AAHM.*

Douglas C-47A Skytrain *(HAS Photo)*

The Skytrain is a short to medium range transport powered by a pair of 1,200-hp Pratt & Whitney R-1830-S1C3G Twin Wasp radial piston engines. It had a maximum speed of 230 mph, a service ceiling of 23,200', and a range of 2,125 miles. *The Complete Encyclopedia of World Aircraft.*

Few aircraft are as well known or were so widely used for so long as the C-47 or "Gooney Bird" as it was affectionately nicknamed. The aircraft was adapted from the DC-3 commercial airliner which appeared in 1936. The first C-47s were ordered in 1940 and by the end of WW II, 9,348 had been procured for AAF use. They carried personnel and cargo, and in a combat role, towed troop-carrying gliders and dropped paratroops into enemy territory. After WW II, many C-47s remained in USAF service, participating in the Berlin Airlift and other peacetime activities. During the Korean War, C-47s hauled supplies, dropped paratroops, evacuated wounded and dropped flares for night bombing attacks. In Vietnam, the

C-47 served again as a transport, but it was also used in a variety of other ways which included flying ground attack (gunship), reconnaissance, and psychological warfare missions. *Information courtesy of the US Air Force Museum.*

The Douglas DC-3 cargo and passenger aircraft was the workhorse of the armed forces for many years. It carried heavy loads to high altitude and was used extensively in the China-Burma-India theater of WWII to fly supplies "over the hump" (The Himalayan mountains). It was used by paratroopers and figured prominently in the European "D" day invasion. There are at least two Skytrains on display in Alaska, including one at Kulis ANG Base in Anchorage and a second at Wasilla, in the Museum of Alaska Transportation & Industry. Another Skytrain that had served in Alaska was last used by the military as an Arctic research laboratory out of Point Barrow Alaska. It is now on display at the Pueblo Weisbrod Air Museum in Colorado. (PWAM). The Dakota was powered by a pair of Pratt & Whitney R-1830-S1C3G Twin Wasp radial piston engines.

Fairchild C-119 Flying Boxcar

The Boxcar is a twin-tailed short-nosed transport aircraft first produced in 1949 as an Assault Transport aircraft. The Flying Boxcar was powered by a pair of 3,500-hp Wright R-3350-85 Duplex Cyclone 18-cylinder radial piston engines. It had a maximum speed of 200 mph, and a range of 2,280 miles. *The Complete Encyclopedia of World Aircraft.*

The C-119, developed from the WW II Fairchild C-82, was designed to carry cargo, personnel, litter patients, and mechanized equipment, and to drop cargo and troops by parachute. The first C-119 made its initial flight in November 1947 and by the time production ceased in 1955, more than 1,100 C-119s had been built. The USAF used the airplane extensively during the Korean War and many were supplied to the U.S. Navy and Marine Corps and to the Air Forces of Canada, Belgium, Italy, and India. In South Vietnam, the airplane once again entered combat, this time in a ground support role as the AC-119G gunship. *Information courtesy of the US Air Force Museum.*

There are three Flying Boxcars working in Alaska, Serial No. N8504X, with Northern Pacific Transport in Anchorage; Serial No. N8504Z, with Evert's Air Fuel, in Fairbanks; and Serial No. N8505A, with Northern Pacific Transport, also in Anchorage.

Fairchild C-123J Provider *(HAS Photo)*

The Provider is a short-range tactical assault transport used to airlift troops and cargo onto short runways and unprepared airstrips. It is powered by two 2,300-hp Pratt & Whitney R-2800-99W Double Wasp 18-cylinder radial piston engines. It has a maximum speed of 245 mph, and a range of 1,470 miles. *The Complete Encyclopedia of World Aircraft.*

Designed by the Chase Aircraft Co., the C-123 evolved from earlier designs for large assault gliders. The first prototype XC-123 made its initial flight on October 14, 1949, powered by two piston engines. A second prototype was built as the XG-20 glider. It was later test-flown, powered by four jet engines. The production version, with two piston engines, was designated the C-123B. Chase began manufacture in 1953, but the production contract was transferred to Fairchild. The first of more than 300 Fairchild-built C-123Bs entered service in July 1955. Between 1966 and 1969, 184 C-123Bs were converted to C-123Ks by adding two J85 jet engines for improved performance. The C-123J transport was equipped with both wheels and skis and a number served with the Alaska ANG until 1979. *Information courtesy of the US Air Force Museum.*

Fairchild OA-10 Thunderbolt II *(Photo courtesy of the USAF)*

The Thunderbolt is a single-seat close-support aircraft powered by a pair of 9,065-lb thrust General Electric TF34-GE-100 turbofans. It has a maximum speed of 439 mph, and an endurance rate of 1 hour and 40 minutes. The Thunderbolt II is armed with a General Electric GAU-8/A Avenger 30mm seven-barrel cannon. *The Complete Encyclopedia of World Aircraft.*

The A-10 is the first USAF aircraft designed specifically for close air support of ground forces. It is named for the famous P-47 Thunderbolt, a fighter often used in a close air support role during the latter part of WW II. The A-10 is designed for maneuverability at low speeds and low altitudes for accurate weapons delivery, and carries systems and armor to permit it to survive in this environment. It is intended for use against all ground targets, but specifically tanks and other armored vehicles. The Thunderbolt II's great endurance gives it a large combat radius and/or long loiter time in a battle area. Its short takeoff and landing capability permits operation from airstrips close to the front lines. Service at forward area bases with limited facilities is possible because of the A-10's simplicity of design. The first prototype Thunderbolt II made its initial flight on May 10, 1972. A-10A production commenced in 1975. Delivery of aircraft to USAF units began in 1976 and ended in 1984. *Information courtesy of the US Air Force Museum.*

General Dynamics F-16 Fighting Falcon *(Photo courtesy of the USAF)*

The Fighting Falcon is a single-seat front-line air-superiority and air-to-ground attack fighter, powered by a Pratt & Whitney F100-PW-220 engine, or by a General Electric F110-GE-100 after-burning turbofan. It has a maximum speed of more than 1,320 mph, a service ceiling above 50,000', and a range of 575 miles. *The Complete Encyclopedia of World Aircraft.*

The Falcon has been nicknamed the "Electric Jet", and it is highly maneuverable. Its strong, light, carbon-epoxy frame can withstand 9 G's of pressure (about the maximum a pilot can take), and computerized "fly-by-wire" controls maximize the F-16's flight characteristics. A side-arm control mounted on an arm-rest helps the pilot keep hold of the stick under high Gs, and head-up instrumentation enables him to keep his eyes on the target. The USAF Thunderbird Air Demonstration Team has been flying the F-16 since 1983. One Falcon is on display at Eielson AFB.

The F-16 evolved from a 1972 USAF Lightweight Fighter (LWF) prototype program which sought a small, lightweight, low cost, air-superiority day fighter designed for high performance and ease of maintenance. It achieved combat-ready status in October 1980. Many foreign nations, including Belgium, Denmark, Turkey, Egypt and Israel, have purchased the F-16. *Information courtesy of the US Air Force Museum.*

Grumman J2F-6 Duck *(Photo courtesy of the US Air Force Museum)*

The Duck is a two or three-seat utility amphibian powered by one 900-hp Wright R-1820-54 Cyclone 9-cylinder radial piston engine. It has a maximum speed of 190 mph, a service ceiling of 25,000', and a range of 750 miles. It could be armed with two 325-lb depth bombs. *The Complete Encyclopedia of World Aircraft.*

The Navy's J2F-6 Duck amphibian was derived from the XJF-1, a Grumman amphibian that flew for the first time in May 1933. Later, Grumman built a variety of JF- and J2F- series aircraft that were used primarily by the Navy, Marine Corps, and Coast Guard, before and during World War II. After the war, air-sea rescue duties assigned to the USAF's Air Rescue Service required special aircraft for overwater missions. So in 1948, the USAF acquired eight surplus Navy J2F-6s for air-sea rescue work. Five were designated OA-12s and sent to Alaska for duty with the 10th Air Rescue Squadron (the other three disappeared from the records and apparently went to an allied country under the Mutual Defense Assistance Program). *Information courtesy of the US Air Force Museum.*

In 1937 the first of 544 Grumman J2F "Ducks" was delivered to the Navy. The J2Fs were utilized in the fleet for anti-submarine operations as well as utility aircraft aboard carriers in a ship-to-shore link. Several were ordered for the Coast Guard as well as a Marine Scouting Squadron to be equipped with machine guns and bomb racks. During World War II, the "Duck" served in a number of operational roles in the Atlantic and Pacific Theaters. A Coast Guard J2F aircraft played an instrumental part in the capture of a secret German radio station in Greenland while J2Fs fitted with depth charges were credited with damaging at least two German submarines in the Atlantic. In the Pacific, a J2F on a photo-reconnaissance mission was credited with damaging two Japanese "Zero" fighters and rescued many downed pilots at sea.

CDR Elmer Stone, USCG, who is best remembered as the pilot of the NC-4 transatlantic flight, also set a world speed record of 192 mph for amphibious planes in a JF-2 (the first version of the Duck series). The NMNA's aircraft (BuNo. 33581) was acquired from Naval Air Station,

Norfolk, Virginia in 1970. *Information courtesy of the National Museum of Naval Aviation.* One is on display at the Alaska Aviation Heritage Museum.

Grumman G-21A Goose (N789)

The G-21 Goose was a high-wing monoplane light amphibious transport powered by a pair of 450-hp Pratt & Whitney Wasp Junior SB radial engines. *The Complete Encyclopedia of World Aircraft.*

It was primarily used for communication and light transport duties. Appearing in 1937, the JRF "Goose" was the first in a long line of amphibian flying boats produced by Grumman Aircraft Corporation for military and commercial use. Equipped with main and tail wheel landing gear, which retracted into the fuselage, the high-wing aircraft was also capable of carrying six to seven passengers. Variants of the "Goose" ranged from the JRF-1 to the JRF-6 series with the first production models being delivered to the Navy in late 1939 and to the Marines and Coast Guard shortly thereafter. Under the Lend Lease Act, 54 of the more than 300 produced were programmed for Great Britain as a navigation trainer. While provisions were made for the carriage of two 250-pound bombs on wing racks, the primary duties within the Navy were as a utility transport, to tow targets, as a photo aircraft, and navigation training. The Coast Guard provided some of them with autopilots and anti-icing equipment for use in northern waters.

Goose No. N789 was in service with the US Navy until being surplused to the US Fish and Wildlife Service in 1956. The immortal Grumman has flown all over Alaska from the Aleutian Islands to the Arctic Ocean throughout its service life. Goose No. N789, was donated to the Alaska Aviation Heritage Museum by the US Department of Interior in 1997 through the efforts of Senator Ted Stevens. *AAHM.*

Lockheed P-38G Lightning *(HAS Photo)*

P-38G10-LO, Serial No. 42-13400 on display at Elmendorf AFB was powered by two turbo-charged 1,325-hp Allison V-1710-51 or 55 engines. The aircraft had a range of 2,400 miles, a service ceiling of 39,000', and a maximum speed of 400 mph at 25,000'. It is armed with four Browning .50 cal machine-guns with 500 rounds each and one Hispano-Suiza 20mm cannon with 150 rounds.

The Lockheed P-38 Lightning was originally designed to meet the 1937 Army Air Corps requirements for a high altitude interceptor. It became one of the most versatile fighters of WWII. It saw action in every American theatre of operations during the war. The Lightning was employed operationally for the first time as a fighter in the Aleutian Islands and achieved its first aerial victory there. A total of 10,038 were built of which 1,082 were G models. Approximately 24 survive today, including the only remaining G-model in the markings of Lt Nesmith's P-38.

On 01 June 1945, Lt Robert L. Nesmith, 54th Fighter Squadron, inadvertently flew his P-38 Lightning into the ground during a training mission in Temnac Valley on the island of Attu. Although shaken, he emerged unhurt. Shortly afterwards, a salvage team removed all useable parts and left the remains of his fighter to the elements. The Alaska Aircraft Historical Society placed the Lightning on the National Register of Historic Planes in 1979. An Air Force maintenance team from Elmendorf AFB visited the site in 1991 and determined that the aircraft could be restored. At this time, the Project Lightning Save Group was formed. After several unsuccessful attempts, the group achieved official approval to recover the P-38, when General McCloud learned of the project and responded "go get it." A joint Air Force, U.S. Fish and Wildlife Service, National Park Service and State Historic Preservation Officer effort resulted in the necessary approval documents. A volunteer recovery and documentation team from the 3rd Wing and the State Office of History and Archeology, supported by helicopters and Lockheed HC-130 Hercules transport aircraft from the 210th Air Reserve Squadron, and the U.S. Coast Guard LORAN Station on Attu, recovered the P-38 in early June 1999. Alaska Air National Guard and 3rd Wing C-130 crews transported the Lightning to Elmendorf AFB where volunteers restored the aircraft with funding provided by the McChord Memorial Foundation. *(Data from a commemorative plaque at the Elmendorf AFB display site).*

Lockheed P-80 Shooting Star *(HAS Photo)*

The Lockheed F-80 Shooting Star was one of American's first single-seat jet fighters. The F-80 was powered by an Allison J33-A-35 turbojet, with a maximum speed of 600 mph and a range of 1,345 miles. The first flight made by an X P-80 was made on 9 January 1944, followed by a P-80 equipped with the J33 engine which was flown 11 June 1944. After June 1946 the Shooting Star was designated F-80. This was the US Air Force's first true jet-powered fighter of the jet air age. *The Complete Encyclopedia of World Aircraft.*

Production delivery began in Aug. 1943. On the 25th of June 1950, the F-80C went to the War in Korea. On the 8th of November, a pilot of an F-80C tangled with a Russian MiG 15 in the first jet-to-jet dogfight and emerged victorious. By the time production halted on the Shooting Star and its various versions including the TF-80C, there had been 1,714 built. Another version was designated as the T-33 and these were used to train the first jet pilots. There were a total of 5,691 T-33s built. The Shooting Star was powered by an Allison J33-A-35 turbojet. *(Information courtesy of the US Air Force Museum).*

P-80 Serial No. 91849 is on display at the Kulis ANG Base.

Lockheed T-33A Shooting Star *(HAS Photo)*

The two-place T-33 jet was designed for training pilots already qualified to fly propeller-driven aircraft. It was developed from the single-seat F-80 fighter by lengthening the fuselage slightly more than three feet to accommodate a second cockpit. Originally designed the TF-80C, the T-33 made its first flight in March 1948. Production continued until August 1959 with 5,691 T-33s built. In addition to its use as a trainer, the T-33 has been used for such tasks as drone director and target towing, and in some countries even as a combat aircraft. The RT-33A version, reconnaissance aircraft produced primarily for use by foreign countries, had a camera installed in the nose and additional equipment in the rear cockpit.

The T-33 is one of the world's best known aircraft, having served with the air forces of more than 20 different countries for almost 40 years. Many were supplied to foreign nations under the Military Aid Program, and are still in use throughout the world. A total of nearly 6,000 were built. The Canadian Forces (CF) used a license-built version with a Rolls-Royce Nene engine. *Information courtesy of the US Air Force Museum.*

T-33A Serial No. 36021 is on display at Elmendorf AFB, and T-33A Serial No. 35403 is on display at Kulis ANG Base. This aircraft was assigned to the Alaska Air Command at Elmendorf AFB, and is painted in the air defence markings of the 1970's. The 3rd Tactical Fighter Wing also flew T-33s from 1974 to 1987 at Clark AFB in the Philippines. T-33 Serial No. 35403 is on display at Kulis ANG Base. T-33A Serial No. 52-9772 is on display in Kenai.

Martin B-10 Bomber *(Photo courtesy of the US Air Force Museum)*

The B-10 was a 4 or 5-seat twin-engine bomber powered by two 775hp R-1820-33 Cyclone nine cylinder radial engines. The bomber had a maximum speed of 213mph and a service ceiling of 25,200', and a range with full bombload of 700 miles. The B-10 was armed with three .3in machine-guns manually aimed from a nose turret, the rear cockpit, and a rear ventral hatch. The bomb load consisted of 1,000lb carried in an internal bay underneath the centre section in the fuselage. The aircraft made its first flight in 1932. The Martin B-10 is thought to be one of the most significant military aircraft for its era, because it came with a variety of new improvements, such as cantilever monoplane wings, flaps, all-metal stressed-skin construction, retractable landing gear, advanced engine cowls, variable-pitch propellers, a fully-glazed cockpit and gun turret, and an internal bomb bay with power-driven doors. At the time of its introduction, the B-10 could fly faster than any of the pursuit fighters then in service. One of these aircraft is in the care of the Alaskaland Pioneer Air Museum, Fairbanks.

The B-10, the first of the "modern-day" all-metal monoplane bombers to be produced in quantity, featured such innovations as internal bomb storage, retractable landing gear, a rotating gun turret, and enclosed cockpits. It was so advanced in design that it was 50% faster than its contemporary biplane bombers and as fast as most of the fighters. When the Air Corps ordered 121 B-10s in the 1933-1936 period, it was the largest procurement of bomber aircraft since WW I. It also ordered 32 B-10 type bombers with Pratt and Whitney rather than Wright engines and designated these B-12s.

General Henry H. "Hap" Arnold once called the B-10 the air power wonder of its day. In 1934, he led ten B-10s on a 8,290 mile flight from Washington, D.C. to Fairbanks, Alaska and back. Although Air Corps B-10s and B-12s were replaced by B-17s and B-18s in the late 1930s, China and the Netherlands flew export versions in combat against Japan. *Information courtesy of the US Air Force Museum.*

McDonnell F-101B Voodoo

The Voodoo was a two-seat all-weather long-range interceptor powered by two 14,880-lb thrust afterburning Pratt & Whitney J57-P-55 turbojets. It had a maximum speed of 1,221 mph, a service ceiling of 40,000' and a range of 1,550 miles. It was armed with two MB-1 Genie missiles with nuclear warhead and four AIM-4C,-4D or 04G Falcon missiles or six Falcon missiles. *The Complete Encyclopedia of World Aircraft.*

Developed from the XF-88 penetration fighter, the F-101 originally was designed as a long-range bomber escort for the Strategic Air Command (SAC) (now known as Strategic Command). However, when high-speed, high-altitude jet bombers such as the B-52 entered active service, escort fighters were not needed. Therefore, before production began, the F-101's design was changed to fill both tactical and air defense roles. The F-101 made its first flight on Sep. 29, 1954. The first production F-101A became operational in May 1957, followed by the F-101C in September 1957 and the F-101B in January 1959. By the time F-101 production ended in March 1961, McDonnell had built 785 Voodoos including 480 F-101Bs, the two-seat, all-weather interceptor used by the Air Defense Command. In the reconnaissance versions, the Voodoo was the world's first supersonic photo-recon aircraft. These RF-101s were used widely for low-altitude photo coverage of missile sites during the 1962 Cuban Missile Crisis and during the late 1960s in Southeast Asia.

The F-101 lineage included several versions: low-altitude fighter-bomber, photo-reconnaissance, two-seat interceptor and transition trainer. To accelerate production, no prototypes were built, the first Voodoo, an F-101A, made its initial flight on September 29, 1954. When production ended in March 1961, nearly 800 Voodoos had been built. Development of the unarmed RF-101, the world's first supersonic photo-recon aircraft, began in 1956 while 35 RF-101As and 166 RF-101Cs were produced, many earlier single-seat Voodoos were converted to the reconnaissance configuration. *Information courtesy of the US Air Force Museum.* One is used as a fire-fighting hulk at Eielson AFB.

McDonnell-Douglas F-4 Phantom II (Elmendorf AFB) *(HAS Photo)*

The two-place Phantom II is an all-weather, multi-role fighter with advanced radar and missile armament. It is powered by a pair of 17,900-lb afterburning thrust General Electric J79-GE-17 turbojets, with a maximum speed of 1,485 mph, a service ceiling of 62,250', and a combat radius of 595 miles. *The Complete Encyclopedia of World Aircraft.*

The armament loaded on a typical F-4C consists of four AIM-7E and four AIM-9B air-to-air missiles, and eight 750 lb. Mk. 117 bombs. The aircraft could also carry two external 370-gallon fuel tanks on the outboard pylons and one ALQ-87 electronic countermeasures (ECM) pod on the right inboard pylon. This was one of the typical armament configurations for the F-4C during the Vietnam War in the summer of 1967.

The Phantom is one of the most versatile aircraft in USAF and USN history, serving in fighter-attack, reconnaissance and interceptor roles. Based on its combat record the Phantom may be considered to be the most significant American fighter to take to the skies in combat since WWII. The USAF and the USN Phantoms scored 72% of all victories over North Vietnam between 1965 and 1973. Phantoms first deployed to PACAF in December 1964. Seven months later, F-4Cs shot down two MiG-17s, marking the first USAF kills of the Vietnam War. Phantoms subsequently operated in the PACAF theatre for ten years. Captain Steve Ritchie made his six kills in a Phantom similar to the aircraft that are on display at Elmendorf AFB.

The two F-4Cs on display at Elmendorf AFB are painted with the markings of the 35th Tactical Fighter Squadron, assigned to the 3rd Tactical Fighter Wing at Kunsan Air Base, Korea, and later stationed at U-Tapao Air Base, Thailand, from 1971-1974. F-4s were flown in Alaska from 1970 to 1980. F-4C Serial No. 64-00890), painted as 66-723 is displayed inside Elmendorf AFB, F-4C Serial No. 64-890 is displayed as a gate guard at the entrance to the AFB at Government Hill Gate.

First flown in May 1958, the Phantom II originally was developed for U.S. Navy fleet defense and entered service in 1961. The USAF evaluated it for close air support, interdiction, and counter-air operations and, in 1962, approved the USAF version. The USAF's Phantom II, designated F-4C, made its first flight on the 27th of May 1963. Production deliveries began in November 1963.

In its air-to-ground role the F-4 carried twice the normal bomb load of a WW II B-17. USAF F-4s also flew reconnaissance and "Wild Weasel" anti-aircraft missile suppression missions. Phantom II production ended in 1979 after over 5,000 had been built—more than 2,600 for the USAF, about 1,200 for the Navy and Marine Corps, and the rest for friendly foreign nations. In 1965 the first USAF Phantom II's were sent to Southeast Asia (SEA). The first USAF pilot to score four combat victories with F-4s in South East Asia was then Col. Robin Olds, a WW II ace. Col. Olds, the aircraft commander, and Lt. Stephan B. Croker, the backseat pilot, scored two of those victories in a single day, on the 20th of May 1967.

The armament loaded on a typical F-4C consists of four AIM-7E and four AIM-9B air-to-air missiles, and eight 750 lb. Mk. 117 bombs. The aircraft is also carrying two external 370-gallon fuel tanks on the outboard pylons and one ALQ-87 electronic countermeasures (ECM) pod on the right inboard pylon. This was one of the typical armament configurations for the F-4C during the Vietnam War in the summer of 1967.

Information courtesy of the US Air Force Museum.

McDonnell Douglas F-15A Eagle *(Photo courtesy of USAF)*

The Eagle is a single-seat all-weather air-superiority fighter powered by two Pratt and Whitney F-100 turbofan engines which produce high performance, high maneuverability, and enable it to quickly achieve Mach 2.5. Each engine has 23,000 pounds of thrust. The Eagle can climb to 50,000 feet in one minute. It is armed with one M61A1 20mm six-barreled cannon and four AIM-9 Sidewinder, four AIM-7 Sparrow or eight AMRAAM air-to air missiles. The Eagle can also carry 6,000 lb of weapons externally. *The Complete Encyclopedia of World Aircraft.*

Eagles were deployed to PACAF in December 1979, and were assigned to the 18th Tactical Fighter Wing (TFW), at Kadena AFB, Japan. The

Eagle replaced the venerable F-4C Phantom and was first assigned to Alaska in 1982. F-15A Serial No 95081 on display at Elmendorf AFB is painted with the markings of the 3rd Wing flagship as it served in the Air Defence Mission for the State of Alaska.

First flown on 27 July 1972, the Eagle began entering the USAF inventory on 14 November 1974. It was the first U.S. fighter to have engine thrust greater than the normal weight of the aircraft, allowing it to accelerate while in a vertical climb. This, combined with low aircraft weight compared to wing area, made the Eagle highly maneuverable. The Eagle has been produced in single-seat and two-seat versions. During Operation Desert Storm F-15Cs conducted counter-air operations over Iraq. They escorted strike aircraft over long distances and scored 36 of the 39 USAF aerial victories during the conflict. The F-15C was also used to search out and attack Scud ballistic missile launchers. *Information courtesy of the US Air Force Museum.*

Noordyn UC-64A Norseman (NC725E)

The UC-64A is a ten-place, single-engine utility transport manufactured by the Noorduyn Aviation, Ltd., Montreal, Canada. The Norseman is powered by one 550-hp Pratt & Whitney R-1340-AN-1 Wasp radial piston engine, and had a maximum speed of 155 mph, a service ceiling of 17,000', and a range of 1,150 miles. *The Complete Encyclopedia of World Aircraft.*

Also manufactured by Canadian Car and Foundry Co., the Norseman was used to transport troops during WWII, the Norseman later joined the US Fish and Wildlife Service before coming to Alaska with Northern Consolidated Airlines in 1951. Interior Airways purchased the aircraft in 1955 to use during the construction of the Distant Early Warning (Dew) Line. The DEW Line was a radar defense system. The aircraft was also used for other bush flying, until it was donated by the Fairbanks North Star Borough, Jim and Dottie Magoffin. *AAHM.*

First flown in 1935, the Norseman was designed for rugged Canadian bush country operations and could be equipped with wheels, floats, or skis. Before WW II, 69 were delivered to the Royal Canadian Air Force as trainers. After service testing seven YC-64s, the U.S. Army Air Forces adopted the aircraft in 1942 as a light transport. Noorduyn produced 762 Norseman for the USAAF before the war ended. Of these, 749 were UC-64As, including three that went to the Navy as JA-1s and six that were equipped with floats for the U.S. Army Corps of Engineers. The last Norseman was produced in late 1959.

Designed for and used in arctic areas, the Norseman also was employed in Europe and the Pacific as well as in the U.S. during the war. On Dec. 15, 1944, a UC-64A disappeared on a flight from England to France with bandleader Major Glenn Miller on board. The aircraft was never found. *Information courtesy of the US Air Force Museum.*

North American T-6G Texan *(HAS Photo)*

The Texan was a two-seat advanced trainer powered by a 550-hp Pratt & Whitney R-1340-AN-1 radial piston engine. It had a maximum speed of 205 mph, a service ceiling of 21,500', and a range of 750 miles. *The Complete Encyclopedia of World Aircraft.*

The AT-6 advanced trainer was one of the most widely used aircraft in history. Evolving from the BC-1 basic combat trainer ordered in 1937, 15,495 Texans were built between 1938 and 1945. The USAAF procured 10,057 AT-6s; others went to the Navy as SNJs and to more than 30 Allied nations. Most AAF fighter pilots trained in AT-6s prior to graduation from flying school. Many of the Spitfire and Hurricane pilots in the Battle of Britain trained in Canada in "Harvards," the British version of the AT-6. To comply with neutrality laws, U.S. built Harvards were flown north to the border and were pushed across. In 1948, Texans still in USAF service were re-designated as T-6s when the AT, BT, and PT aircraft designations were abandoned. To meet an urgent need for close air support of ground forces in the Korean Conflict, T-6s flew "mosquito missions" spotting enemy troops and guns and marking them with smoke rockets for attack by fighter-bombers. *Information courtesy of the US Air Force Museum.*

Texan Serial No. 453015A on display at Kulis ANG Base is on loan from the USAF Museum and is painted in the markings of AT-6 Serial No. 34555, which was the first Texan assigned to the Alaska ANG in February 1953. This specific machine served the Alaska ANG until it crashed near Eagle River on 21 October 1955.

North American F-86E Sabre *(HAS Photo)*

The F-86 Sabre is a single-seat all-weather/night fighter-bomber/interceptor powered by one 7,500-lb thrust afterburning GE J-47-13 turbojet engine. It had a maximum speed of 707 mph, a service ceiling of 54,600', and a range of 835 miles. It was armed with six .50 cal nose-mounted machine-guns. *The Complete Encyclopedia of World Aircraft.*

The Sabre such as the one on display at Kulis ANG Base was one of the most famous combat aircraft of its day. The first model flew on 01 October 1947, and many hundreds were soon on order. In the Korean War, the F-86Es with their slotted wings and powered "flying tails" were expertly flown against the technically more advanced MiG-15s, establishing a marked superiority over the pilots from the other side.

The Sabre was the first US fighter to be developed using captured German swept-wing technology. It had been discovered that the build-up of shock waves on the leading-edge of the wing could be postponed by sweeping it aftwards, so that the angle formed by the wing's leading edge and fuselage was less than 90 degrees. The Sabre was the USAF's first swept-wing fighter. It was the primary opponent of the formidable MiG-15 during the Korean War.

Many Sabre variants were built, ranging from the standard day-fighter to the heavily modified Sabre Dog. The Sabre was powered by a General Electric J47-GE-17B or –33 turbojet. The F-86D (known briefly as the YF-95A) made its first flight on December 22, 1949. It was developed as an all-weather interceptor version of the famed F-86A, the airplane that won supremacy of the skies from the MiG 15 during the Korean War. The F-86D was used during the 1950s, both in the U.S. and overseas, to guard against possible air attack. In all, 2,506-Ds were produced. The F-86D was known for two historic firsts. It was the first USAF airplane to have all-rocket armament, and the first all-weather interceptor to carry only one person for operating the radar fire control system as well as piloting the airplane. It also had the unique distinction of succeeding itself in setting a new world's speed record: 698.505 mph on the 19th of November 1952 and 715.697 mph on the 16th of July 1953. As a day fighter, the airplane saw service in Korea in three successive series (F-86A, E, and F) where it engaged the Russian-built MiG-15. By the end of hostilities, it had shot down 792 MiGs at a loss of only 76 Sabres, a victory ratio of 10 to 1. More than 5,500 Sabre day-fighters were built in the U.S. and Canada. The airplane was also used by the air forces of 20 other nations, including West Germany, Japan, Spain, Britain, and Australia. *Information courtesy of the US Air Force Museum.*

Northrop F-89J Scorpion *(HAS Photo)*

The Scorpion was a two-seat, twin-engine, all-weather fighter-interceptor designed to locate, intercept, and destroy enemy aircraft by day or night under all types of weather conditions. It carried a pilot in the forward cockpit and a radar operator in the rear who guided the pilot into the proper attack position. The Scorpion was powered by a pair of after-burning thrust Allison J35-A-35,-33A,-41, or–47 turbojets, which gave it a maximum speed of 636 mph, a service ceiling of 49,200', and a range of 2,600 miles. The Scorpion was armed with 104 70mm rockets in wingtip pods or 27 rockets plus 3 Falcon missiles. *The Complete Encyclopedia of World Aircraft.*

The first F-89 made its initial flight in August 1948 and deliveries to the Air Force began in July 1950. Northrop produced 1,050 F-89s. On the 19th of July 1957, a Genie test rocket was fired from an F-89J, the first time in history that an air-to-air rocket with a nuclear warhead was launched and detonated. (That particular F-89J presently survives as a gate guard for the Montana ANG in Great Falls, Montana). Three hundred and fifty F-89Ds were converted to "J" models, which became the

Air Defense Command's first fighter-interceptor to carry nuclear armament. *Information courtesy of the US Air Force Museum.*

The F-89J Scorpion on display at Elmendorf AFB is painted with the markings of the 54th Fighter Interceptor Squadron, and was assigned to Ellsworth AFB, South Dakota, from 1952 to 1960. In 1957, while flying the F-89, the 54th won the Hughes Trophy for best overall interceptor squadron in the Air Force. The squadron later moved to Elmendorf and was assigned F-15C fighter aircraft.

Piasecki (Vertol) CH-21B Shawnee Helicopter *(HAS Photo)*

The CH-21B "Shawnee" was designed as a troop and cargo-carrying transport helicopter, powered by one 1,425-hp Wright R-1820-103 Cyclone radial piston engine driving two separate rotor blades. It had a maximum speed of 131 mph, a service ceiling of 7,750', and a range of 400 miles. *The Complete Encyclopedia of World Aircraft.*

CH-21B Serial No. 53-04369 on display outside the hospital entrance to Elmendorf AFB was also known as the " Work Horse," "Retriever," or "Mule," but has more often been referred to as the

"Flying Banana." Another CH-21 is on display at Wasilla in the Museum of Alaska Transportation and Industry. The H-21 made its first flight in April 1952. The aircraft was originally designed to transport men and cargo but was later adapted for the rescue of personnel and for assault operations under combat conditions. Normally having a crew of two (pilot and copilot), the H-21 could carry either 20 fully equipped troops or 12 litter patients. In addition to serving with the USAF, the H-21 was supplied to the U.S. Army, the French navy, the Royal Canadian Air Force and the West German Air Force. *Information courtesy of the US Air Force Museum.*

Sikorsky HO4S Helicopter *(Photo courtesy of the US Air Force Museum)*

The HO4S is a variant of the H-19 and S-55 helicopters. It was used to transport men and equipment. The HO4S-3 variant was used for anti-submarine operations and as a search and rescue helicopter. The H-19 Horse was powered by a Pratt & Whitney R-1340-57 engine. With its all-important winch and strong 600-horsepower engine, the S-55 proved an invaluable tool in the business of saving lives. Whether over open seas, in mountains or other inconvenient places, there weren't many locations a Sikorsky S-55 wouldn't be of use. One is on display in the Alaskaland Pioneer Air Museum at Fairbanks.

Sikorsky S-60/CH-54B Flying Crane (Tarhe)

On 25 March 1959, an S-60 flying crane, using the engines and rotor system of the S-56/H-37, made its first flight. This led to the turbine powered, purpose built S-64 Skycrane, designated CH-54A Tarhe. Its first flight was on 9 May 1962. Nine test aircraft were built, and they saw service with the Army beginning in 1965. 60 were built, and they were powered by two 4,500-shp P&W T73 engines. The Tarhe's empty weight was 19,234 lb and maximum loaded weight was 42,000-lb. The seat for the load-master looked rearward under the fuselage. The later CH-54B had 4,800-shp engines and additional lifting capacity; 29 were built. The Tarhe holds several international records for payload-to-height and time-to-height. About 10 commercial variants were also sold, but they were very expensive to operate. *Information courtesy of the American Helicopter Society.*

Though none are currently on display in Alaska, two of these helicopters saw extensive military service throughout the state, and one assisted with lifting the PBY from its remote crash site to the AAHM.

Stinson L5 Sentinel

The Stinson L5 was produced for the U.S. Army Air Corps as a liaison and communications aircraft. It was powered by one 185-hp Lycoming O-435-1 flat-six piston engine. It had a maximum speed of 130 mph, a service ceiling of 15,800', and a range of 420 miles. *The Complete Encyclopedia of World Aircraft.*

Many were produced for the British and operated in Burma under the Lend Lease Plan. In Alaska, the Stinson L5 was used by the 10th Rescue Squadron at Elmendorf and was the first aircraft used by the Alaska Civil Air Patrol. This aircraft was donated by Chuck Hughes in 1993. *AAHM.*

Stinson AT-19 Reliant (N79548)

The Reliant is a four-seat cabin monoplane powered by one 245-hp Lycoming R-680-6 radial piston engine. The aircraft had a maximum speed of 135 mph, a service ceiling of 15,500', and a maximum range of 645 miles. *The Complete Encyclopedia of World Aircraft.*

This model on display at the *AAHM* was built by the Americans for the British during WWII. It was the last of the famous "gullwing" design for Stinson. After WWII the Stinson became available to the commercial market in the United States. Northern Consolidated, Wien Airlines, Alaska Airlines and Munz Northern Airline all used AT-19s. This aircraft was purchased from the Planes of Fame Museum in Chino, California by Don Rogers and Bob Wagstaff of Anchorage and donated to the aviation museum, where it was fully restored by museum volunteers. *AAHM*

V-1/JB-2

The JB-2 is a U.S. made copy of the famous German V-1 surface-to-surface pilotless flying bomb first used against England on June 12-13, 1944. The airframe for the JB-2 was built by the Republic Aviation

Corporation and the engine by the Ford Motor Company from drawings prepared at Wright Field, using dimensions taken from the remains of several V-1s brought from Germany.

About 1,000 JB-2s were built for the Army and Navy. Production delivery began in January 1945, but it was cancelled on VJ Day. The first one to be test flown in the U.S. was launched at Eglin Field, Fla., in October 1944. Just before the end of the war, JB-2s were placed aboard an aircraft carrier en route to the Pacific for possible use in the proposed invasion of the Japanese home islands. Although the JB-2 was never used in combat, it provided valuable data for the design and construction of more advanced weapons. *Information courtesy of the US Air Force Museum.*

Other Aircraft on Display in Alaska

1928 Fairchild FC-2W (NC7034)

The FC-2W was a high wing monoplane used for aerial survey work. It was generally similar to the FC-2 but was intended to be primarily a cargo-carrier. It had modified windows, an increased wingspan and area, and a more powerful engine. The FC-2W was a more powerful version of the FC-2L, which also served during the same period. The latter version had an Armstrong Siddeley Lynx VIB powerplant while the "W" boasted the more powerful Pratt & Whitney Wasp A. FC-2W's were produced wholly by Fairchild. The *AAHM*'s aircraft was operated by Bob Reeve in the 1940s and used by him on famous glacier flights. This FC2W2 is one of only six known to exist. *AAHM*.

1928 Stearman C3B (NC5415)

In 1929, Ben Eielson purchased this single-engine biplane Stearman from Noel Wien for the newly established Alaskan Airways, Inc. The C3B was powered by a 220-hp Wright J-5 Whirlwind radial engine. In November 1929, pilot Eielson and his mechanic, Earl Borland, were lost while flying a Hamilton Metalplane to Siberia in an attempt to the stranded fur ship, Nanuk. With only 40 hours flight time, novice aviator Harold Gillam flew the Stearman on an extraordinary search for the downed men. NC5415 was among the first to land on Mount McKinley in 1932, and also made historic flights to arctic villages with diphtheria serum in 1931 with pilot Joe Crosson. *AAHM*.

1928 Hamilton Metalplane (H47) (NC7791)

In 1928, the Hamilton Metalplane was the 21st aircraft purchased by Northwest Airlines, based in St.Paul, Minnesota. Wien Alaska Airlines purchased the Metalplane in 1937 and brought it to Alaska. This single-engine biplane aircraft is the same model flown by pioneer aviator Ben Eielson, when he crashed near North Cape, Siberia in 1929. The museum's example is one of two remaining in existence today. After an accident in 1939, the Wien brothers sold the Metalplane and it belonged to various aircraft collectors in the lower 48 states before being acquired by *AAHM*. Noel Wien used a sister ship NC10002, to make the first flight from North America to Asia in March 1929. *AAHM*.

1929 Travel Air 6000B NC8159

The Travel Air is a three-seat biplane powered by one 165-hp Wright J-6 radial piston engine. It had a maximum speed of 120 mph, a service ceiling of 13,000', and a range of 650 miles. The *AAHM*'s Travel Air came to Alaska in 1939 with "Mudhole" Smith's Cordova Air Service and later belonged to Peck and Rice Airways in Bethel. A number of pioneer aviators owned NC8159, including Albert Ball, Fred Goff and Al Jones. Restoration including the original 1929 EDO floats is underway. *AAHM*.

1929 Bellanca CH300 Pacemaker (NC168N)

The Pacemaker was a six-place cabin monoplane manufactured under license by Canadian Vickers, Montréal. The basic Pacemaker was powered by a Wright J-6-9 engine; the Pacemaker 30 and 31 variants were powered by a Wright J-6E-9 engine. The *AAHM*'s aircraft first flew in Alaska in 1934 with Star Airways. It crashed in Rainy Pass in 1946 and was retrieved by Warren Magnuson several years ago. Acquired by the museum through a trade, the Bellanca is one of six known to exist. *AAHM*.

1929 Keystone Loening Commuter (KI 84)

This two-seat biplane aircraft was flown to Alaska in 1946 by former Governor Jay Hammond. The Loening is one of two existing today. The aircraft was dubbed "The Old Patches" by Hammond. *AAHM*.

1929 Ford Trimotor (wreckage) (NC8034)

The Trimotor was a commercial transport powered by three 420-hp Pratt & Whitney C-1 or SC-1 Wasp 9-cylinder radial piston engines. It had a maximum speed of 150 mph, a service ceiling of 18,500', and a range of 550 miles.

Based on a series of all–metal cantilever monoplanes designed by Bill Stout, the Ford Motor Company developed and produced the famed RR–5 "Tri–Motor" aircraft in 1926 at a new factory in Detroit, Michigan. The prototype of the new design was the largest all–metal aircraft built in America up to that time. It provided accommodations for 8 passengers and featured corrugated aluminum clad covering of the fuselage, wing and tail surfaces for rigidity purposes. Attesting to its design strength are films taken during early air shows of the RR–5 performing aerobatics that included loops, slow rolls, spins and hammerhead stalls.

In addition to gaining quick acceptance by airlines in the United States and elsewhere, nine of them were purchased for use by the Navy and Marine Corps between 1927 and 1931 as passenger and cargo carriers. One model was fitted with pontoons and tested as a torpedo bomber, while another was utilized by CDR Richard E. Byrd for the first historic flight over the South Pole.

As they phased out from commercial and military use in the mid–1930s, the "Tri–Motors" were bought by private owners for primitive cargo/passenger use in Latin and South America (selling price approximately $3,800). The few remaining in active use more than 60 years after their introduction are worth over a million dollars each. *Information courtesy of the National Museum of Naval Aviation.*

The *AAHM*'s trimotor was the first of its type to come to Alaska. Operated by aviation pioneers, Frank Dorbant and Don Glass, a.k.a. Ptarmigan Airlines, the Ford arrived in Anchorage in 1934. After groundlooping at Flat, Alaska in the fall of 1934, the Ford was used as a tool shed for the Willow Creek Mine, Fuselage and wing center section were recovered and brought to the museum in 1990 with helicopter assistance of the Alaska National Guard & Markair C-130. *AAHM.*

1931 American Pilgrim 100B (NC709Y)

The single-engine biplane Pilgrim came to Alaska in 1936 with Alaska Air Express and was later owned by Star Airlines, Alaska Airlines and eventually the Ball brothers Fish Company. As the last remaining Pilgrim, NC709Y is on the US National Register of Historic Objects. *AAHM.*

1933 Stinson Senior (N3831)

The Stinson senior was an upgraded version of the single-engine three or four-seat Stinson Junior high-wing monoplane. The *AAHM*'s Stinson Senior arrived in Alaska in early 1940 flown by Gene Effler. Orin Hudson of Nondalton, a.k.a. Hudson Air Service, purchased it in the early 1950's. He flew this aircraft several hundred hours on floats, wheels and skis to fly freight and passengers and the U.S. mail to area villages. Wien Alaska Airlines, Collins Air Service and Aho Flying Service were among other companies utilizing the Stinson SR type. *AAHM.*

1934 Waco YKC (NC14066)

The Waco YKC is a four or five-place single-engine biplane with fixed landing gear, and powered by a 285-hp Jacobs engine. Waco No.

NC14066 was flown to Alaska in 1939 by "Red" Flensburg to establish Dillingham Air Service. It was also owned by Bud Branham, who operated Rainy Pass Lodge in the Alaska Range. The aircraft is a gift from Mrs. Elmer Rasmussen. *AAHM*.

1935 Bellanca Sr. Pacemaker

The Pacemaker was a six-place cabin monoplane manufactured under license by Canadian Vickers, Montréal. The basic Pacemaker was powered by a Wright J-6-9 engine; the Pacemaker 30 and 31 variants were powered by a Wright J-6E-9 engine. One of two examples surviving, the Senior Pacemaker is an improved version of the CH300 Bellanca Pacemaker. Although only the bare airframe survives today, this aircraft once flew with Pollack Air Service and Alaska Airlines. *AAHM*.

1937 Spartan 7-W Executive (NC17602)

The Spartan 7-W Executive is a five-seat low wing monoplane powered by a 400-hp Wasp Junior engine. The *AAHM*'s aircraft was purchased Dupont Corp by the Morrison Knudsen Construction Company in February 1943. Pilot Ian Brady flew it to Alaska for survey work during the construction of the Alaskan Highway and military houses throughout the territory. In August 1944, the Spartan lost an engine and crashed near the Tetlin River. The wreckage was retrieved in 1994 by museum volunteers. *AAHM*.

1937 Stinson SR-9 Gullwing (NC18419)

The SR-9 is a four-seat cabin monoplane, powered by one 245-hp Lycoming R-680-6 radial engine with a maximum speed of 135 mph, a service ceiling of 15,500', and a range of 645 miles.

The *AAHM* Stinson SR-9 is one of Alaska's most historical surviving aviation relics, and was owned and flown by some of the most famous of Alaska aviation's pioneers. Initially brought to Alaska by Linius McGee, the SR-9 Gullwing was sold to Oscar Winchell (a.k.a. "The Flying Cowboy"), by Ray Peterson (a.k.a. "King of the Bushpilots"), Albert Ball of Western Alaska Airlines, and the legendary Bill Munz of Munz Northern Airlines in Nome. Inherited by Dick Galleher of Nome, the unrestored airplane was acquired for the *AAHM* collection in 1988. *AAHM*.

1937 Fairchild 24-G

The Fairchild 24-G was a three or four-seat utility cabin monoplane powered by one 145-hp Warner Super Scarab Series 50 7-cylinder radial piston engine. It had a maximum speed of 130 mph, a service ceiling of 16,500', and a range of 475 miles.

The Fairchild 24-G used by the Civil Aeronautics Administration, now called the Federal Aviation Administration (FAA) during the 1930's and 1940's in Alaska. The Fairchild 24-G was a type flown by Alaska CAA pioneers Clarence Rhode & Jack Jefford. The museum example was fully restored to flying condition by *AAHM* volunteers in 1997. *AAHM*.

A Brief History of the Air War in the Pacific during WWII

The air war for the United States in World War Two would essentially begin with the Japanese raid on Pearl Harbor. At the time, the eyes of the world were focused on the war in Europe, while the Japanese had increasingly begun to find themselves trapped in circumstances that made war with the United States a likely necessity. Japan had been at war with China for some time, but this war consumed a great deal of the island's scarce resources. The fall of France enabled Japan to exert political pressure on the French colony of Indochina to supply it with rice, coal, and rubber which helped to sustain the fighting in China, as well as permitting Japan access to ports and airfields. The Japanese gradually expanded their power southward until July 1941, when the exploitation of Indochina gave way to armed occupation. The Roosevelt administration reacted by imposing a freeze on Japanese assets in the United States. This course of action was also adopted by Great Britain and the Dutch government in exile. The impounding of funds prevented Japan from purchasing oil from the United States or from the Dutch colonies, which left only distant sources such as Latin America and the Middle East as possible suppliers of fuel for their war in China. In contrast, the oil of the poorly defended Netherlands East Indies lay near at hand, although any move in that direction would require the neutralization or conquest of the Philippines. That option, in turn, could only be assured by the defeat of the American Pacific Fleet, which Roosevelt had shifted during 1940 from San Pedro, California, to Pearl Harbor, Hawaii, to deter Japanese aggression in the western Pacific. Instead of discouraging Japanese ambitions, the freeze of funds and resulting embargo on the sale of oil convinced the more militant Japanese leaders that war with the United States was all but inevitable.[10]

America had begun to build up its defences in the Pacific, but it also hoped that if it had to go to war with Japan, the Soviet Union would permit American bombers to shuttle between Luzon in the Philippines and Vladivostock, attacking the Japanese home islands en route. No such agreement was forthcoming, as the Russians were already reeling back from the German onslaught and were unwilling to risk a two-front war by antagonizing Japan.[11]

Late in 1940, the War Department began dispatching modern fighters to Pearl Harbor, where the Pacific Fleet stood by to discourage Japan's southward expansion. The principal mission of the Hawaiian Air Forces, commanded since November 1940 by Major-General Frederick L. Martin, was to protect the Pearl Harbor naval base. Shortly after General Martin's arrival, Navy aircraft carriers began delivering Curtiss P-36 Hawks and Curtiss P-40 Warhawk fighters. By December 1941 the Hawaiian Air Forces had 99 P-40s along with 39 of the older P-36s and 14 of the obsolete Boeing P-26 Peashooter fighters. In addition, a small contingent of bombers operated from the island of Oahu, which consisted of 33 obsolete Douglas B-18 Bolos, 12 modern Douglas A-20A Havoc attack aircraft, and 12 Boeing B-17D heavy bombers.[12]

General Martin had two major concerns about the security of his air force. The first was the dispersal of his aircraft, the second was reconnaissance. The shortage of available land frustrated his plan to disperse the aircraft on small airstrips throughout the Hawaiian chain. The lack of long-range bombers or patrol aircraft prevented the execution of a joint search plan drawn up in collaboration with the naval air command. Based

---

[10.] Bernard C. Nalty, *Reaction to the War in Europe*, pp. 195-196.
[11.] Ibid, pp. 196-197.
[12.] Ibid, p. 198.

on the assumption that the "most likely and dangerous form of attack on Oahu would be an air attack,' the plan called for "daily patrols as far seaward as possible through 360 degrees," a task that could not be carried out, except briefly during an emergency, with the aircraft available.[13]

At that time, the defenders of Hawaii believed that the only real danger to their aircraft lay in the threat of sabotage. This caused the Army to concentrate its aircraft at the main bases, and to park them together to ease in the task of guarding them, instead of dispersing them and building revetments to reduce the danger from air attack. The real danger would come from the skies, because Japan had already decided to launch a carrier attack against Pearl Harbor if the Americans made no concessions by the deadline that Japan had set.[14]

Before the situation came to a head, the United States Army Air Force (USAAF) was established in June 1941. The specific aim of the USAAF was to direct the activities of the existing military air elements of the US Air Corps and the Air Force Combat Command. The USAAF's commander at that time was Major General H.H. Arnold, who had assumed the office of the Chief of the Air Corps in 1938 on the death of General Westover. Under his command the USAAF had begun to expand, and by the 1st of December 1941 it had a personnel establishment of some 23,000 officers, 16,000 cadets, 275,000 enlisted men and 12,000 aircraft. This brought the total of existing American Air Forces to eight, four of which were based within the continental limits of the United States, while one each was located in Hawaii, the Philippines, Alaska and the Caribbean.[15]

During this period of increased tension, American cryptanalysts were decoding Japanese diplomatic messages and charting the breakdown of peaceful relations between the two countries. This intelligence was called "Magic", and it provided evidence of the increased likelihood of war. The

---

[13.] Ibid, pp. 198-199.
[14.] Ibid, p. 199.
[15.] James J. Haggerty and Warren Reiland Smith, *The U.S. Air Force*, p. 44.

Japanese could strike almost anywhere in the Pacific, and at the same time, the distribution of Magic information was poorly coordinated. Decoded messages that might have sounded alarms in Hawaii failed to reach the commanders there, and the warnings that did arrive were not shared between the Army and the Navy.[16]

By this time, however, Japan's Vice-Admiral Chuichi Nagumo had already been at sea since 22 November 1941. He was in the progress of leading a massive Japanese task force which included six aircraft carriers out of Tankan Bay in the Kurile Islands, on a mission that history would come to know as the "Hawaii Operation." Nagumo's flagship, the *Akagi*, originally designed as a cruiser, had been converted into a heavy carrier to subvert the restrictions on battleships that had been imposed following the Washington Conference (1921-22). In addition to the *Akagi*, Nagumo's command included the heavy carriers *Kaga*, *Soryu*, and *Hiryu* and two light carriers, *Zuikaku* and *Shokaku*, as well as two battleships and two heavy cruisers in the support force under Vice-Admiral Gunichi Mikawa. The scouting force, under Rear Admiral Sentaro Omori, consisted of a light cruiser and nine destroyers. Three submarines patrolled in advance and along the flanks of the armada. They were supported by a supply force of eight tankers for refueling along the task force's 3,000-mile route from Tankan Bay to a point in the Pacific Ocean about 200 miles north of Oahu, Hawaii.[17]

On board the 6 carriers were 423 aircraft of which 353 were to be used in the attack. The air assault would be led by Commander Mitsuo Fuchida, an experienced naval aviator with 25 years service who had trained these aircrews. The remainder of the aircraft were held in reserve, or patrolled over the ships of the strike force.[18]

[16.] Bernard C. Nalty, *Reaction to the War in Europe*, pp. 199-20.

[17.] Edward Jablonski, Air War, Tragic Victories, Doubleday & Company Inc., Garden City, New York, 1971, p. 3.

[18.] Ibid, p. 9.

The Hawaii Operation had been planned by Admiral Isoroku Yamamoto, Commander in Chief of the Combined Japanese Fleet. Yamamoto had been educated at Harvard, and had served in Washington in the Japanese embassy from 1925 to 1927. His superior was General Hideki Tojo, who had become Premier of Japan on 18 October 1941. Tojo was a veteran of the Japanese war in China, which had been in progress since 1931. In September 1940, Japan had signed a Tripartite pact with Italy and Germany, which stipulated that should any member of the pact be attacked by any nation not then at war (in this case, as far as Japan was concerned, specifically the United States), the others would assist them. Yamamoto opposed the pact with the Axis, but he was overruled. Not long after these events unfolded, President Franklin D. Roosevelt placed an embargo on scrap iron and steel "to all nations outside the Western Hemisphere except Britain." This embargo caused a great deal of anger in Japan, and on the 8th of October 1940, Japan's Ambassador to the United States, Admiral Kichisaburo Nomura, formally protested by referring to the embargo as "an unfriendly act."[19]

When Tojo came to power, Yamamoto was directed to implement the "Hawaii Operation." Yamamoto's contention was, "if Japan must go to war, then the United States fleet must be eliminated from the beginning of the war." The thought behind this plan was, with the USA out of the battle, the Japanese would be free to seize the rich islands to the south, and then set up a defensive perimeter that would run from the Japanese Islands out through the Pacific around the Marshall and Gilbert Islands, on to New Guinea and the East Indies and up into Burma. From this defensive bastion, the Japanese believed they could then batter the British and what remained of the US forces until they called for a negotiated peace. These

---

[19.] Ibid, pp. 4-5.

plans, however, depended on a completely successful outcome from the Hawaii Operation.[20]

Not one of Nagumo's more than 30 ships was spotted during the 11-day voyage from Tankan Bay to the launch point about 200 miles north of Oahu. From here, on the 7th of December 1941, the Japanese attacked Pearl Harbor with 353 carrier-based aircraft (183 aircraft in the first wave and 170 in the second wave) striking successive blows against Navy ships in Pearl Harbor, at Ford Island and at Kaneohe, and against the Army's Hickam and Wheeler Air Fields. Within three hours after having dropped the first bombs on Pearl Harbor, the Japanese had sunk or badly damaged eight battleships of the US Pacific Fleet and ten lesser ships. 2,335 American servicemen were killed and another 1,143 were wounded for the combat loss of 29 Japanese aircraft and their crews. The Hawaiian Air Force had more than a third of its aircraft destroyed and a great number of others damaged to varying degrees, leaving about 80 aircraft still able to fly. More than 200 airmen were killed and another 300 were wounded.[21]

A number of sites on Oahu are still marked by the remains of the Japanese raid. Petty Officer First Class Takeshi Hirano was shot down by defensive ground fire during a strafing run at Hickam Field. His aircraft was a Mitsubishi A6M2 Zero, operating from the IJN aircraft carrier Akagi, and he crashed at Fort Kam, hitting a palm tree and killing four men on the base. The remains of his aircraft were shipped to the Lockheed Aircraft Company in Burbank, California for restoration and evaluation. Later, his aircraft was put on display in a number of War Bond drives in the US.[22]

[20.] Ibid, pp. 5-6.
[21.] Bernard C. Nalty, *The Army Air Forces in Desperate Battle*, 1941-1942, Winged Shield, Winged Sword, Vol I, p. 202.
[22.] Earnest Arroyo, *Pearl Harbor*, Metro Books, NY, NY, 2001, p. 141.

Lieutenant Mimori Suzuki flying from the aircraft carrier Kaga, was shot down by Chief Gunner's Mate Harry L. Skinner from the destroyer USS Bagley. Suzuki was flying his aircraft over the Southeast Loch to make his torpedo run at about 40' to 50' above the water when he was hit and crashed.[23]

15 of the 29 aircraft lost in the raid on Pearl Harbor by the Japanese were from the IJN aircraft carrier Kaga. She lost 4 Zero fighters, 5 Kate bombers, 6 Val dive-bombers and all 31 of the aircrew in those aircraft.[24]

At about 0900 on the 7th of December, Lieutenant Fusato Iida led a squadron of nine Zero fighters from the IJN aircraft carrier Soryu in a second strike on Kaneohe NAS. Hit by ground fire, Iida's fighter began streaming fuel. The squadron leader realized he could not make it back and signaled for the others to return to the carrier. That morning before takeoff, Iida told his comrades that if he could not return, he would crash his aircraft into an enemy target. He therefore banked back and flew towards the Kaneohe armory. As he dove down, Iida came under heavy machine-gun fire and was fatally hit. His aircraft crashed into a hill, skidded across and piled up on an embankment, where a remembrance place marker is positioned today.[25]

A number of P-40 Warhawks were shot up at Bellows Field, a small airbase primarily used for training that was located on a stretch of white coral sand along the South East coast of Oahu. A squadron of 12 P-40s had flown in on the 6th of December for gunnery practice. The following morning, nine Zeros strafed the airplanes parked on the runway. Lieutenant Hans. C. Christiansen was killed as he climbed into the cockpit of his P-40. Two other pilots, 2Lt. George A. Whitman and 1Lt. Samuel W. Bishop, also attempted to take off. Whitman managed to get airborne with two Zeros on

---

23. Ibid, p. 141.
24. Ibid, p. 142.
25. Ibid, p. 143.

his tail, but was hit and killed 50' off the ground, sending the P-40 crashing into the beach. Taking off seconds behind Whitman, Bishop could not gain altitude and was also shot down. His airplane crashed into the ocean about a half-mile from shore. Despite a leg wound, Bishop managed to swim to shore. His Mae West life jacket had kept him afloat. Both pilots were awarded the Silver Star for bravery.[26]

When the Japanese aircraft attacked Wheeler Field, pilots George S. Welch and Kenneth M. Taylor hoped in Taylor's car and sped off to the north shore's Haleiwa Field, where their squadron was located. Upon arrival, they found that their ground crews already had their P-40s armed and warming up. The two officers took off immediately and winged south, towards Ewa Field, where they spotted a dozen or so enemy aircraft attacking the marine airfield. Diving into the formation, they each downed two Val dive-bombers in the melee, while Taylor inflicted damage on two others. Low on fuel and ammunition, they returned to Wheeler Field for rearming and refueling. Minutes later they were ready to scramble. As he followed Welch into the air, Taylor was fired on by a Val on his tail and wounded in the arm and leg. Returning to help Taylor, Welch jumped on the enemy plane and scored his 3rd kill. Despite his wounds, Taylor continued to fly. The two pilots pursued the retreating Japanese raiders, with Taylor damaging another Val and Welch tallying a 4th kill. For their heroism in the skies above Pearl Harbor, both men received the Distinguished Service Cross.[27]

When the Japanese attacked Hickam Field on the 7th of December 1941, the AAF had 231 aircraft at the bases on the islands. By nightfall, 64 of them had been completely destroyed and only 79 aircraft remained in commission. As indicated, only six pilots of the 47th Pursuit Squadron

---

[26.] Ibid, p. 116.
[27.] Ibid, p. 47.

from Haleiwa got airborne during the second Japanese raid in Curtiss P-40 Warhawks and P-36 Hawks. A number of aircraft from the carrier *Enterprise* were also shot down during the battle, including SBD Dauntless dive-bombers, and several Wildcat fighters. In all however, the Japanese lost only 29 out of the several hundred attacking planes.[28]

2,340 servicemen were KIA during the attack, (2,107 navy and 233 Army & AF). Word of the raid had already reached Washington when Japanese emissaries delivered a note severing diplomatic relations. On the 8th of December 1941, President Roosevelt issued a declaration of war against Japan. Three days later, Germany and Italy, Japan's Axis partners, declared war on the United States.[29]

Right from the time of its entry into the Second World War in 1941, the United States found that much of its air fleet had been destroyed not only at Pearl Harbor, Hawaii, but also at other bases in Asia. The people of the United States rallied to the cause and their military and industrial forces worked hard to recover rapidly. In due course the massive US industrial capacity was brought to bear on the task of gearing up for war. American industry would eventually produce over 300,000 aircraft for the war effort. (The industrial engines of Germany and Japan combined never managed to produce two-thirds of that number). Most American aircraft were heavily armed and relatively reliable. The incredible number of advanced aviation designs that were produced also contributed to the rapid development in aviation technology. Many aircraft that had been considered new and advanced at the beginning of the war were removed from front line duties because they had quickly become vulnerable and obsolete. Technological developments would lead the participants in the air war from the propeller age into the jet and nuclear age before the war ended. In the process, the Army Air Corps, which had been renamed the

---

[28] Bernard C. Nalty, *The Army Air Forces in Desperate Battle, 1941-1942*, p. 214.

[29] Ibid, p. 202.

United States Army Air Forces (USAAF), became a vital tool that was used to sweep the skies of enemy aircraft between 1942 and 1945.[30]

A few hours after the attack on Pearl Harbor, another Japanese force launched an air and sea attack against the Philippines, where the Far East Air Force had 38 B-17's and 90 fighters. Although many got airborne, many were also lost. 18 of the B-17's were destroyed and a similar number of the pursuit fleet were cut down. On the 9th and 10th of December, five B-17's of the 14th Bombardment Squadron attacked a Japanese convoy steaming toward Luzon. One of the B-17C's piloted by Captain Colin Kelly bombed and appeared to have damaged the heavy Japanese cruiser Ashigara. Although Kelly's aircraft was shot down by a swarm of enemy fighters and he was killed in the action, he remained at the controls long enough for six of his crew-men to escape by parachute.[31]

General Claire L. Chennault of the American Volunteer Group, the Flying Tigers, had flown for the Chinese government against the Mitsubishi A6M Zero-Sen or type 0 fighter. He had already warned United States aviators about the capabilities of this fast, nimble, long-range airplane, and noted that Jiro Horikoshi, the aircraft's designer, had given it the ability to turn more tightly than any allied aircraft. As the Flying Tigers had already discovered and others were soon to learn, the American pilots had to avoid dog-fights with the Zero and instead use their greater diving speed and overwhelming firepower to defeat it. The Zero was vulnerable, however, because it obtained its range and quickness by sacrificing armor, structural strength, and self-sealing fuel tanks. It did not take many hits to knock it down.[32]

The first Japanese Zero captured intact was found on Akutan Island. Its pilot died after a forced landing following a Japanese attack on Dutch

---

[30]. Daniel J. Kaufman, *United States Air Force*, p. 3.
[31]. Bernard C. Nalty, *The Army Air Forces in Desperate Battle*, 1941-1942, p. 214.
[32]. Ibid, p. 214.

Harbor on the 3rd and 4th of June 1942. This attack had been conducted by 16 fighter and torpedo bombers flying from the Imperial Japanese Navy (IJN) aircraft carrier Ryujo. The Zero's wreckage was found inverted with the pilots body five weeks later. An evaluation and recovery team quickly shipped the aircraft back to the continental US for study.[33]

At the time of Pearl Harbor, Japanese flying schools were producing about 2,000 army and navy combat pilots a year. In contrast, the U.S. Army Air Forces alone graduated some 11,000 pilots in 1941. Japan then had about 2,700 modern aircraft, equally divided between its army and navy. This force was overwhelmingly superior to the few hundred aircraft, many of which were obsolete, that the Allied forces in the Pacific were able to gather together in 1941 and 1942. Many of the Japanese pilots were already experienced in combat from the war with China. The end result was that Japan had a clear advantage in men and equipment at the start of the war. Clearly, however, Japanese leaders did not foresee and anticipate the need to replenish the men and machines that would be lost in the war with the United States. As indicated earlier, Admiral Yamamoto had tried to explain to his leaders that Japan could not hope to match the American potential industrial output, but he was over-ruled.[34]

Over the next few months, the Japanese swept through the Pacific against little or no opposition. The Japanese carved out an empire that swallowed up Malaya, the Netherlands East Indies, the Philippines, and the islands of the central Pacific. The Dutch surrendered on the 2nd of March. Wake Island was taken, Burma was lost and by mid-May 1942, the Japanese had overrun the Bataan peninsula and the island fortress of

---

[33]. John Hale Cloe, *The Aleutian Warriors, A History of the 11th Air Force and Fleet Air Wing 4, Part 1*, Anchorage Chapter, Air Force Association and Pictorial History, Missoula, Montana, 1990, p. 134 and p. 175.

[34]. James J. Haggerty and Warren Reiland Smith, *The U.S. Air Force*, p. 76.

Corregidor, the last two outposts on Luzon. American forces withdrew to Australia, while Douglas A-24 dive-bombers, Boeing B-17s and Curtis P-40s which were scattered from Hawaii to Java continued the fight.[35]

The one bright spot at this time in 1942, was a raid against the Japanese homeland which was carried out on the morning of the 18th of April 1942 by 16 North American B-25B Mitchell medium bombers from the 17th Bombardment Group. The bombers were launched from the aircraft carrier Hornet, and were led by Lieutenant-Colonel Jimmy Doolittle. The plan was to bring the Hornet, protected by Navy Task Force 16 (which included the carrier Enterprise), into position 400 miles east of Tokyo and to send the bombers from the carrier on a strike against the heart of the enemy. Unfortunately, the task force was still 800 miles off Japan on the 18th of April when it encountered Japanese patrol craft. The task force commander, Vice Admiral William F. Halsey, Jr., proposed that Doolittle dispatch his bombers at once, even though the Hornet was more than 100 miles farther from the Japanese coast than planned. Doolittle agreed and directed his team to conduct a premature take-off. Doolittle then proceeded to lead his 16 aircraft on a low-level surprise attack against Tokyo. 13 of the raiders bombed Tokyo, smashing factories, docks, oil dumps and supply depots, while the other three attacked Kobe and Nagoya. A lucky, unpredicted tailwind had made it possible for all the aircraft to reach the China coast, where the crews bailed out or crash landed (except for one, which ended up landing safely in Vladivostock, Russia). Doolittle then made his way to Chungking, where he was picked up by an American transport. Three of Doolittle's 79 airmen died in crash landings

---

[35.] Bernard C. Nalty, *The Army Air Forces in Desperate Battle, 1941-1942*, p. 216.

or parachute jumps, and the Japanese patrols took eight of the Tokyo raiders prisoner. Of those captured, three were executed by firing squad and another died in confinement, but the other four survived a brutal imprisonment.[36]

The air resources to follow up this attack on the homeland of Japan were severely lacking. On the 31st of December 1941 the United States air arm had only 332 B-25 Mitchells and B-26 Marauders in its inventory to wage a worldwide war against the combined might of the Axis forces of Germany, Italy and Japan. They were only able to build and deploy another 1,500 in all of 1942. The total number of B-17 Flying Fortresses and B-24 Liberators on the 31st of December 1941 was 287, although an additional 1,900 were constructed within the year. On the brighter side, the prototypes of the B-29 Superfortress long-range bomber first flew in 1942, and American aircraft production steadily increased.[37]

Throughout 1942 in the Pacific, heavy air battles were fought over the numerous Japanese held island strongholds. Heavy and medium bombers of the 5th Air Force struck against major enemy strongpoints, while fighters, most notably the Lockheed P-38 Lightning, fought to control the skies, while the 13th Air Force supported operations against Japanese forces on Guadalcanal and New Georgia with heavy bombardment and reconnaissance missions.[38]

Throughout the beginning of the war in the Pacific, the Japanese carried the assault to the allied forces with deadly effect. They had carried out landings on the islands of Guam and Luzon 10-11 December. On the 20th of December they attacked the British battleship *Prince of Wales* and the battle-cruiser *Repulse* sinking them using Japanese Mitsubishi G4M Betty torpedo-bombers off the coast of Malaya, in the Battle of the Gulf of

---

[36.] Ibid, p. 202.
[37.] Ibid, p. 202.
[38.] Bernard C. Nalty, *The Army Air Forces in Desperate Battle, 1941-1942*, p. 205.

Siam. Between the 18th of January and the 17th of March 1942, the Japanese forces occupied Burma. The British forces in Singapore surrendered on 15 February. On the night of the 23rd of February 1942, a Japanese submarine shelled an oil refinery near Santa Barbara, California. This attack led to an alert watch for Japanese aircraft, and resulted in the firing of 1,400 rounds of anti-aircraft ammunition at weather balloons. On the 8th of March 1942, Japanese forces occupied Java.

The first week of April was particularly disastrous. On the 5th of April 1942, Japanese Admiral Nagumo brought his combined fleet into the Indian Ocean to strike at the British-held Island of Ceylon. Britain's Admiral Somerville with the Far Eastern Fleet (including the carriers *Formidable* and *Indomitable*) set out to engage the Japanese fleet with the heavy cruisers *Cornwall* and *Dorsetshire*. Aircraft from the Japanese carriers *Akagi*, *Soryu* and *Hiryu* and the heavy cruiser *Tone*, spotted and sank both ships. The following day, the 6th of April 1942, a Japanese force consisting of the light carrier *Ryujo*, five heavy cruisers, a light cruiser and four destroyers under the command of Vice Adm. Jisaburo Ozawa sank 23 Allied merchant ships in the Bay of Bengal.

On the 7th of April, the Japanese forces occupied Sumatra. On the 8th of April, Admiral Nagumo's fleet led by the battleship *Haruna* attacked Admiral Somerville's fleet and sank the British aircraft carrier *Hermes* (which had left its aircraft behind at China Bay), with the loss of 307 personnel. In other engagements the Australian destroyer *Vampire* was also sunk. Aircraft from the Japanese carriers *Akagi* and *Hiryu* sank several other ships and also engaged a number of British shore based Allied aircraft. The loss of the Hermes was also the first sinking of an aircraft carrier by ship-based planes.

The Navy had its hands full later in the spring, with the Battle of the Coral Sea which took place between the 4th and 8th of May 1942. During this engagement, the Japanese carriers *Shoho*, *Shokaku* and *Zuikaku* with a large strike force moved into the Coral Sea. The American carriers *Yorktown* and *Lexington* attacked the Japanese invasion fleet North of the

Lowside Archipelago. The *Shoho* was sunk on the 7th of May, and the *Shokaku* was damaged. The *Lexington* was also sunk during this battle (the US had 543 casualties). The Japanese lost 43 of 69 aircraft, the Americans lost 33 of 82 aircraft. This was also the first sea battle in history where the surface ships engaged in combat did not exchange a shot, as the battle was conducted completely by aircraft.

In the ground war, the surrender of Corregidor (Philippines) took place on the 8th of May.

The next major sea battle followed a month later, with another American victory at the Battle of Midway which was fought between the 3rd and 7th of June. The Japanese Imperial Fleet lost four aircraft carriers, *Akagi, Kaga, Soryu* and *Hiryu*, and the heavy cruiser *Mikuma*, to American aircraft operating from the carriers *Enterprise, Hornet* and *Yorktown* on the 4th of June. The US fleet lost the carrier *Yorktown* and the destroyer *Hammann*. By the end of the battle, the Japanese had lost 3,500 men, and the Americans had lost 307. More than 300 Japanese aircraft and 147 American aircraft were destroyed. This battle is considered the turning point in the war in the Pacific.

On the 7th of August, US forces landed on the island of Guadalcanal, part of the Solomon Islands. During the multiple land and sea battles on and around Guadalcanal Island, the Japanese carrier *Ryujo* was sunk on the 24th of August, and the American carrier *Enterprise* was damaged on the 25th of August. On the 15th of September, the American carrier *Wasp* was torpedoed and sunk enroute to Guadalcanal. More sea battles followed, and on the 26th of October, the American carrier *Hornet* was sunk, along with the destroyer Porter during the Battle of Santa Cruz. In this action the Japanese carriers *Shokaku* and *Zuiho* were also damaged.

The first major night battle on Guadalcanal took place on the night of 12/13 November 1942. During this battle, a Japanese fleet led by the warships *Hiei* and *Kirishima* accompanied by a destroyer squadron engaged an American cruiser/destroyer task force and fought each other to a standstill. The Japanese lost the battleship *Hiei* and two destroyers, the

Americans lost four destroyers and two cruisers and suffered more than 700 casualties. A second night battle followed, and during this engagement, the American warship *Washington* (with the *South Dakota* withdrawing due to a loss of power after an engagement with Japanese cruisers and destroyers) engaged the Japanese warship *Kirishima*, which was accompanied by cruisers and destroyers.

In the fall of 1942, the Japanese submarine I-25 twice launched a small float-plane to drop incendiary bombs on the Oregon forests, setting one insignificant fire. The Japanese also launched more than 9,000 hydrogen-filled paper balloons, which soared aloft from Honshu in Japan's islands between November 1944 and May 1945. They were intended to catch prevailing winds and to release high-explosives or incendiary devices over American territory. Roughly 285 balloons are known to have reached the United States, depositing their weapons (with little effect) along the West Coast, although a few penetrated as far inland as Nebraska, Iowa and even Michigan. The only known casualties were six picnickers who were killed when they accidentally detonated a bomb that had landed near Bly, Oregon.[39]

Women contributed a great deal of expertise to the wartime Army Air Forces. President Roosevelt signed a bill creating the Women's Army Auxiliary Corps (WAAC) on the 15th of May 1942. The WAAC was later redesignated the Women's Army Air Corps. In January 1945, the number of women serving in the WAAC reached 29,323, of whom about 20% served outside the continental United States. Many performed administrative tasks, more than 1,200 became mechanics and 20 qualified as aircrew members for non-combat flights. Women pilots were assigned to ferry aircraft and other flying duties in the United States and two such groups of civilian volunteers merged into the Women Airforce Service

---

[39.] Ibid, p. 205.

Pilots (WASP). Under the command of their director, Jacqueline Cochran, the WASPs grew to number 1,900,of which 1,074 completed flying training. 37 died in accidents and another 36 sustained injuries ferrying aircraft and towing gunnery targets. The WASPs were disbanded in December 1944.[40]

In the Alaskan region, Japanese troops had occupied Kiska in the Aleutian Island chain on the 12th of June 1942. The 11th Air Force headed by Major General William O. Butler fought to drive the Japanese forces out of the Aleutian Islands. The 11th Air Force provided air support to Operation Landgrab, which culminated in the 11th of May 1943 invasion of the island of Attu. The capture of this island gave the 11th Air Force a base from which its medium bombers could launch attacks against the northern Japanese islands, with the first of these strikes taking place on the 10th of July. Kiska was taken without opposition on the 15th of August 1943.[41]

With a few important exceptions, the Air Forces relied throughout the war on variations of the types of aircraft that were in hand in December 1941. Some 12,600 B-17 Flying Fortresses and more than 18,000 B-24 Liberators served throughout the conflict. The A-26 Invader was a variant of the A-20 Havoc, of which over 7,000 were produced.

North American B-25 Mitchell and Martin B-26 Marauder variants continued in service through 1945, along with 3,000 Bell P-63 King Cobras, which were a super-charged and more powerful variant of the 10,000 P-39 Airacobra fighter's produced. The last of 14,000 Curtis P-40 Warhawks rolled out of the factory in 1944, and almost 10,000 Lockheed P-38 Lightning fighters entered service with their production ending in 1945. The six-ton Republic P-47 Thunderbolt fighter made its debut in

---

[40.] Ibid, p. 254
[41.] James J. Haggerty and Warren Reiland Smith, *The U.S. Air Force*, p. 80.

1942, and the five-ton long-range North American P-51 Mustang followed shortly afterwards, although it did not acquire its Merlin engines until 1943. Other new aircraft that appeared during the war included about 700 twin-boom Northrop P-61 Black Widow night-fighters, and about 3,000 Curtis-Wright C-46 Commandos, about 1,000 Douglas C-54 Skymasters and 14 Lockheed C-69 Constellation transports. The combination of numbers of aircraft and improvements in their variations in allied air power proved to be decisive.[42]

After a series of incredibly hard-fought battles, the Japanese evacuated Guadalcanal on the 8th of February 1943. The air assaults continued over and against the Japanese strong points of New Guinea, Buna, Wewak, Salamaua and Lae. Bougainville in the Solomon's was successfully attacked by two groups of B-24's based at Guadalcanal, 48 B-25's and 148 Navy and Marine Corps torpedo and dive bombers based at Munda and a further force of fighters and miscellaneous aircraft in a combat force of 650 planes, all under the command of General Twining. The air assault began on the 18th of October 1943 and continued through November. On the 13th of November, another campaign was initiated against the Gilbert and Marshall Islands in the Central Pacific, using the 7th Air Force under Major General Willis Hale and later Major General Robert Douglass Jr. The 7th Air Force flew hundreds of sorties against places like Tarawa, Makin, Wotje, Jaluit, Maloelap and Kwajalein. After the fall of Tarawa in November 1943, the 7th set up bases there for further strikes against Japanese positions in the Marshall Islands.[43]

The 5th and 13th Air Forces together with Navy, Australian and New Zealand aircraft, conducted devastating attacks against New Britain through January and February 1944, carrying out almost 6,000 sorties.

[42.] Ibid, p. 243.
[43.] Ibid, p. 86.

On the 31st of January 1944, American forces landed on the Marshall Islands. In February, American warships *New Jersey* and *Iowa* (with cruisers and destroyers in support) engaged the Japanese CL (training) warship *Katori* and its supporting destroyers at Truck Lagoon. Further assaults were carried out by the 5th Air Forces P-38's, B-24's, B-25's and A-20's against Hollandia in March 1944, wiping out Japanese air strength in the area. It was in Hollandia that the AAF produced its all-time highest-ranking fighter ace, Captain Richard Ira Bong, who scored more than 27 kills to top WWI ace Eddie Rickenbacker's score.[44]

Laconic and unassuming, Bong compensated for his allegedly poor gunnery with outstanding eyesight and a willingness to fly very near his target. After he topped Rickenbacker's score, he was reassigned from the 5th Air Force to advanced combat instruction. Taking new pilots on practice flights in the Southwest Pacific (in P-38 Lightnings), he bent the rules and bagged another 13 enemy aircraft to score a total of 40 kills by the war's end.[45]

Throughout 1944 and early 1945, U.S and Allied bombers continuously pounded factories and supply lines in Japan, sometimes in round-the-clock operations. Civilian populations were also attacked with the aim of destroying civilian morale and convincing their enemy leaders to concede defeat. Besides the strategic bombing campaign, U.S. tactical fighters engaged Japan's air force in a variety of missions which included bomber escort, interdiction (preventing enemy forces from timely arrival at the battle area), and air superiority.[46]

[44.] Ibid, p. 90.

[45.] Bong died test flying a Lockheed P-80 Shooting Star after the war. Edwards Park, *Fighters, The World's Great Aces and Their Planes*, Barnes & Noble Books, New York, 1990, p. 140.

[46.] Daniel J. Kaufman, *United States Air Force*, p. 4.

Between the 20th and the 23rd of May 1944, American forces landed in New Guinea. A few weeks later, on the 14th of June, allied landings were carried out on the Island of Saipan. Shortly afterwards, on the 19th of June 1944, the Battle of the Philippine Sea was fought. This Japanese and American naval battle is also known as the "Mariana's Turkey Shoot." The Japanese carrier *Hiyo* is sunk and the Japanese lost 480 aircraft, while the Americans lost 130 aircraft. More American landings followed on the 21st of July on the island of Guam and on the 20th of September at Leyte in the Philippines. AAF units had been reorganized for the assault against the Philippines, with the 5th and 13th Air Forces being combined into the Far East Air Forces under General Kenney. General Whitehead took over the 5th Air Force and the 13th came under the command of Major General St. Clair Streett.

On the 20th of October 1944, the American 6th Army waded ashore, supported by 5th Air Force P-38's. By the end of the year, the 5th had shot down 314 enemy aircraft in the vicinity of Leyte, for the loss of 16 of their own. MacArthur's troops invaded Mindoro, south of Manila on the 15th of December and then Lingayen on the main island of Luzon on the 9th of January 1945.[47]

During the Battle of Leyte Gulf which took place between the 22nd and the 25th of October 1944, the Japanese lost a total of 26 ships including four carriers, the *Chitose, Chiyoda, Zuikaku,* and *Zuiho* and the two super-battleships *Musashi* and *Yamato*. The Americans lost six ships including the carriers *Princeton, Saint Lo* and the *Gambier Bay*, which were sunk on the 24th of October. This battle marked the appearance of Japanese

---

[47] Ibid, pp. 90-92.

Kamikaze aircraft (the *Saint Lo* was their first victim). During the Battle of the Surigao Strait (part of the Battle of Leyte Gulf), the US warships *West Virginia, Tennessee, California, Maryland* engaged the Japanese warships *Yamashiro* and supporting vessels. The *Pennsylvania* was unable to fire due to poor fire control but the *Mississippi* fired two salvos. The US force was supported with a substantial number of cruisers and destroyers. The Japanese warship *Fuso* was sunk by destroyer torpedoes without engaging the battleships. The Japanese warships *Yamato, Nagato, Kongo,* and *Haruna* accompanied by strong cruiser and destroyer forces sank the American carriers in the Battle of Surigao Strait.

The Philippine island of Palawan was invaded on the 28th of February 1945, making its valuable airfields available for use. Okinawa fell on the 21st of June 1945. The 5th Air Force joined the 7th in the Ryukyus and both initiated an all out attack on Japanese shipping, as well as on enemy installations in China and on the Japanese homeland itself.[48]

The American carrier *Ommaney Bay* was sunk on the 4th of January 1945 by Japanese Kamikaze attack in Lingayen Gulf. On the 23rd of January, the Burma road to China was reopened. Assaults on the Japanese holdings were carried out, with US forces besieging and capturing the Island of Corregidor between the 16th of February and the 1st of March. Between the 19th of February and the 16th of March, American forces also assaulted and captured the Japanese held Island of Iwo Jima. The American aircraft carrier *Franklin* was badly damaged by a Japanese air attack on the 21st of March.

Shortly afterwards, the Battle 1945 Battle of Okinawa took place between the 1st of April and the 21st of June 1945. The war at sea was no

---

[48.] Ibid, p. 96.

less intense, with the Japanese super-battleship *Yamato* being sunk near the Island of Okinawa with the loss of 2,488 sailors on the 7th of April 1945. Even so, Kamikaze pilots managed to damage the U.S. carrier *Hancock*. On the 14th of April, American forces took back Bataan in the Philippines. On the 11th of May, the American aircraft carrier *Bunker Hill* was severely damaged in a Japanese air attack. First Allied naval bombardment of the Japanese coastlands took place on the 14th of July 1945. Coincidentally, two days later on the 16th of July 1945, the first US atomic bomb is tested at Alamogordo, New Mexico.

The start of 1945 had marked the beginning of an all-out strategic bombing attack on the home islands of Japan, using the new "very heavy" bomber, the Boeing B-29 Stratofortress. The B-29's initially operated out of China with the 20th and 21st Bomber Commands. The Marines took the strategic island of Okinawa in March 1945 after four weeks of bloody fighting. This provided the B-29's with an emergency landing area as well as a base from which P-51 Mustang fighters could escort the B-29's to Japan.[49]

By July 1945, the B-29 force in the Mariannas had grown to almost 1,000 bombers. On the 6th of August, a B-29 of the 20th's 509th Composite Group took off from the island of Tinian with the most destructive bomb load in history. Six hours and 30 minutes later at 08:15 in the morning, the *Enola Gay*, piloted by Colonel Paul W. Tibbetts Jr., dropped a nuclear bomb nicknamed Little Boy on the city of Hiroshima.[50] A ball of fire appeared in the sky, and a mushroom cloud of smoke and debris came writhing upward. At the base of the cloud, a com-

---

[49]. Ibid, p. 100.

[50]. Colonel Tibbetts was offered the mission and accepted it in Colorado Springs. HQ AFSPC/HO, 08 December 2000.

bination of blast, fire, and lethal radiation killed at least 70,000 people, and leveled the heart of the city.[51]

The destruction of Hiroshima did not compel Japan to immediately surrender. President Truman described the weapon as the "force from which the sun draws its power," and he warned Japan that it would face a "rain of death from the air, the like of which has never been seen on earth." In spite of this, the badly divided Japanese government did not act. At 10:58 on the morning of the 9th of August, the B-29 named *Bock's Car* commanded by Major Charles W. Sweeney, dropped a second A-bomb nicknamed Fat Man (originally intended for Kokura), on Nagasaki. The bomb exploded at the right altitude but some two miles wide of the mark. The nature of the hilly terrain below helped reduce the effect of the blast although as many as 35,000 died in the mushroom cloud that devastated this large city. Still the Japanese deliberated, although Emperor Hirohito realized that the situation was hopeless. President Truman had suspended the air war on the 11th of August, but when the Japanese surrender was not immediately forthcoming, he ordered its resumption.[52]

[51.] Bernard C. Nalty, *Victory Over Japan, Winged Shield, Winged Sword*, Vol I, p. 364.

In an atomic bomb, a non-nuclear explosive charge is used to bombard fragments of fissile material, which thus reach a critical mass and spark off a chain reaction in a fraction of a second. The USSR (14 Jul 1949), Great Britain (1952), France (13 Feb 1960), China (1964), India (1974) Israel, South Africa, India and Pakistan test weapons of their own in the years following. On 01 Nov 1952, the first thermonuclear H-bomb is exploded in the USA. The A-bomb uses the fission of heavy nuclei, while the H-bomb uses light nuclei. The USSR (12 Aug 1953), Great Britain (1957), China (1967) and France (1968) all explode H-bomb devices in turn. The detonation of the first atomic bomb in modern times marked 1945 as year one of the atomic era.

[52.] Ibid, p. 364.

On the 14th of August 1945, the 20th Air Force staged the heaviest one-day air assault of the Pacific war, when 828 bombers escorted by 186 fighters, rained 6,000 tons of incendiary and demolition bombs on what remained of Japan's industrial capacity. President Truman announced the unconditional surrender of the Japanese government before the last B-29 had returned.[53]

The cost of the war (in both the European and Japanese theatres of operation) had been heavy. 45,000 United States airmen were killed, another 18,000 wounded, and more than 40,000 were taken prisoner. In addition, the contribution of air power to the war was called into question. Enemy war industries proved far more resilient than strategists expected, and civilian morale withstood waves of bombing.[54]

The advent of nuclear weapons in 1945 meant sweeping change. The atomic bombs that the Army Air Corps dropped on the Japanese cities of Hiroshima and Nagasaki in August 1945, killed about 100,000 people. The bombings did, however help to bring an end to the war, possibly saving millions of Allied soldiers lives that could have been lost in the invasion of the Japanese homeland.[55]

---

[53]. James J. Haggerty and Warren Reiland Smith, *The U.S. Air Force*, p. 102.
[54]. Daniel J. Kaufman, *United States Air Force*, p. 6.
[55]. Ibid, p. 6. As early as October 1939, Leo Szilard, a Hungarian-born physicist who had fled Germany when the Nazis came to power, sought to prod President Roosevelt into action on a project which at that time had overtones of science fiction-the developmen of an atomic bomb. Bernard C. Nalty, Reaction to the War in Europe, Winged Shield, Winged Sword, p. 174.

Korean War Notes

Those who thought that the development of nuclear weapons had brought an end to conventional warfare were proved wrong with the onset of the "Korean War" (1950-1953). This war involved much the same type of combat that was typical at the height of World War II. First, the US Air Force destroyed what limited infrastructure the North Koreans had, then it pursued a policy of interdiction. This meant making use of the allied air power of the United Nations (UN) to stop the movement of weapons and soldiers by the North Koreans and their Chinese allies against the South Koreans. Much of the industrial base supporting the North Koreans was located in China and Russia, which were countries that were off-limits to U.S. bombing. In many ways, the air war in Korea was a smaller version of air war in World War II. The major development for the Air Force during the war was the extensive use of new jet fighters. Even so, nearly 1600 airmen were killed in action during the Korean War.[56]

At the outset of the air war in Korea the USAF used North American F-51 Mustang and F-82 Twin Mustang propeller driven fighters, along with a few squadrons of Lockheed F-80 jet fighters, Douglas B-26 Invaders and B-29 Superfortresses. As the war progressed, other aircraft used in Korea included the Republic F-84 Thunderstreak and the North American F-86 Sabre. On the 1st of September 1951, the Communist forces initiated an all-out campaign designed to gain air superiority over Korea. It is estimated that the Communist forces were equipped with about 1,250 aircraft, including well over 500 of the highly-maneuverable, Soviet-built

---

[56.] Ibid, p. 8.

Mikoyan-Gurevich MiG-15s. The MiG-15 was far superior to all USAF aircraft in the theater at that time with the exception of the North American F-86 Sabre, of which the FEAF had only 105 then on the ground. Furious air battles took place over North Korea, with a lot of action taking place in the area between the Yalu and Chongchon Rivers, a sector, which became known as "MiG Alley." USAF F-86 pilots substituted skill and training for their lack of force in numbers, and shot down enough MiGs to negate the threat they posed. On the 23rd of June 1951, the Soviets proposed negotiations toward a truce in Korea and the UN accepted.[57]

In spite of the negotiations that ensued, a war of interdiction continued until an Armistice was signed on the 27th of July 1953. The lack of a firm resolution to the issue however, has resulted in the fact that although there is an Armistice, a peace treaty does not exist to this day. Because the problem has still not been resolved, 27 years later large numbers of American air and ground forces are continuing to carry out assignments to protect the peace in Korea.

>According to Edwards Park, a fighter pilot, Korea had given the new USAF a chance to show its stuff as its F-86 Sabres dueled with the very similar MiG-15s. The fighter jocks developed combat formation techniques that paid off handsomely. Speed was now too high for more than four planes to fly a squadron mission. The planes spread wide enough to keep four pairs of eyes always searching the sky, yet close enough for wingmen to read their leader's large squadron numbers. These wingmen dropped back a bit in attack, so their guns could bear on the target. They crossed under their leaders when necessary to keep the whole sky under close surveillance.[58]

[57.] James J. Haggerty and Warren Reiland Smith, *The U.S. Air Force*, p. 120.
[58.] Edwards Park, *Fighters*, p. 166.

MiG pilots were generally less aggressive that the Americans, but their planes could fly about 4,000 feet higher than the F-86s. Combats were brief: sight the enemy, climb and turn toward him, hit, run, break back up toward the sun, and hit again if possible. Aces were hard to come by. James Jabara was the first to pass the magic five mark, and was shipped home to boost morale. In early 1953, with more targets in "MiG Alley," a heavily contested air corridor over North Korea, Jabara came back for more, got nine in eight weeks and ended up as one of the war's top scorers. The war's leading ace was Joseph "Mac" McConnell, who seemed intent on showing his buddies what a former navigator could do. Once when he was downed by flak and picked out of the sea, he flew again the next day. His final score was 16 kills.[59]

The Korean War was supposedly the last major conflict in which guns were used in airplanes. Combat in that theatre proved that a pilot flying at sonic speed needed a weapon that could hit the target at the moment he knew it existed. And he needed to know it existed before he could see it. Science had the answers: miniaturized and sophisticated detectors and homing missiles.[60]

[59.] Ibid, pp. 166-171.
[60.] Ibid, p. 171.

VIET NAM DATA

Because the USAF had spent much of the 1950s training and equipping itself for a nuclear conflict, it found itself ill-prepared when the United States became heavily involved in the Vietnam War (1959-1975) in 1964. The restrictions in the Vietnam conflict were similar to what the USAF had undergone during the Korean War, in that the American and Allied forces of Australia and Korea were not allowed to bomb countries outside the Vietnamese borders who were actively aiding the enemy's war effort. In addition, U.S. aircraft faced a new enemy in Vietnam: thousands of surface-to-air guns and missiles fortified around key enemy sites. These air defenses brought down hundreds of planes and killed many aircrews. Some U.S. aircraft, such as the light and fast Republic F-105 Thunderchief were designed to carry nuclear weapons and required substantial modifications to face the rigors of daily combat missions.[61]

Other aircraft that became well known in the Vietnam War include the Martin B-57 Canberra, the McDonnell F-101 Voodoo, and the McDonnell F-4 Phantom.[62]

Americans pitted all their hottest fighters against enemy MiGs in Vietnam, and quickly learned that real missions have little to do with theory. Two aircraft, the McDonnell F-4 Phantom II and the Republic F-105 Thunderchief carried out most of the combat missions against the Mikoyan-Gurevich MiG-17 Fresco, MiG-19 Farmer, and the MiG-21 Fishbed. There were some serious difficulties, in that the Phantom was so

---

[61] Daniel J. Kaufman, *United States Air Force*, p. 10.
[62] McDonnell F-4 Phantoms are on display at Elmendorf AFB.

big that it could be seen before its pilot saw the enemy. To make up for this, they soon learned to fly in elements, their planes at least half a mile and perhaps several miles apart. They learned to skim the ground beneath the radar's sweep, utilizing a handy mountain line (one of which was nicknamed "Thud Ridge"), refueling when they had to from the trailing hose of a flying tanker. They learned to cope with the Russian-built surface-to-air missiles (SAMs) that were their worst foe. A good pilot would climb when he saw the smoke of a SAM, then dive more suddenly than the SAM could.[63]

The Air Force pilots who scored the first combat kills in the Viet Nam war flew McDonnell F-4C Phantom II's, knocking down two MiG-15s on the 10th of July 1965 (the Navy followed with two more on the 17th of July). Three USAF flyers became aces. Two of them, Steve Ritchie and Charles DeBellevue, scored four victories together and one each with other partners.[64] Geoffrey Feinstein achieved his five kills as a radar intercept officer with four different pilots. The Navy also had some success with the Phantom II. Navy pilot Randall Cunningham and his radar-intercept officer William Driscoll killed three MiG's in one day, thus becoming the Vietnam air war's only American "ace" team.[65]

The Air Force also proceeded to direct its offensive effort toward conducting close air support in the dense jungle terrain, transporting troops, and in trying to destroy enemy supply lines which originated in North Vietnam. Much like the experience the Air Force had with the UN in Korea, the use of air support to cut supply lines was relatively ineffective. In 1973, near the end of American involvement in the Vietnam War, the Air Force began to experiment with its first "precision-guided bombs,"

---

[63]. Daniel J. Kaufman, *United States Air Force*, p. 10.

[64]. The Phantom in which Ritchie scored his first and sixth kills is on display at the USAFA.

[65]. Ibid, pp. 188-191.

which could reliably strike very close to their intended target. A more controversial tactic was deployed in Operation Ranch Hand, in which the United States dropped millions of gallons of herbicides (plant killers) such as Agent Orange in an effort to destroy trees and plants that gave the enemy cover. The use of herbicides sparked charges that the United States was violating international norms against using chemical weapons in war, and many of the herbicides were later found to cause birth defects and rare forms of cancer in humans.[66]

Through much of the war, the Air Force's bombing campaign was guided by a doctrine known as escalation. The idea behind the use of escalated bombing was that if the enemy made concessions, the bombing would be reduced or eased, and if they proved intransigent at the negotiation table, the bombing would be stepped up. The result of this policy was that sometimes, in the middle of what were major bombing campaigns, the USAF would be ordered to cease the bombing in the hope that this would induce the North Vietnamese to negotiate. Unfortunately, the lull was usually used by the North Vietnamese to repair damaged areas, bring in supplies, and build more air defenses, thereby blunting some of the more damaging effects of the bombing campaigns.[67]

Escalation was sometimes effective, however. The USAF achieved some of its greatest successes during the "Linebacker" operations, which took place primarily between May and December 1972. These operations involved massive B-52 bombing raids against North Vietnamese cities and military facilities. Although the U.S. lost 15 B-52s during these operations, North Vietnamese peace negotiators did return to the peace talks in Paris, France, after the bombing ended. The Air Force realized that it had

---

[66.] Daniel J. Kaufman, *United States Air Force*, p. 11.
[67.] Ibid, p. 12.

trained for one war: strategic nuclear war against an industrialized enemy, but instead had fought a tactical battle against an undeveloped nation. The Air Force's efforts in the war were often hobbled by limitations on targets, but by the end of the war the Air Force had destroyed virtually all significant military targets. By war's end the Air Force had dropped over 5 million metric tons (over 6 million U.S. tons) of bombs on the country, more than three times the tonnage dropped in World War II. The North Vietnamese won the war despite the heavy bombing, again calling into question the value of strategic bombing. Over 2,600 U.S. airmen were killed during the Vietnam War.[68]

[68.] Daniel J. Kaufman, *United States Air Force*, p. 12.

POST VIET NAM MILITARY BUILDUP

Throughout the post Vietnam era of the 1970s and 80s, the commanders within the USAF worked hard to create a new generation of fighters and bombers that could elude enemy defenses. This was primarily a response to the heavy losses of aircraft and their aircrew to the antiaircraft gunfire and missiles in Vietnam. One of the results of this initiative was the development of the Lockheed F-117 Nighthawk fighter in 1982, and the Rockwell B-1 Lancer bomber, which was first deployed in 1985. The B-1 was followed in 1993 by the Northrop Grumman B-2 Spirit bomber. The F-117 Nighthawk proved to be generally capable of penetrating deep into enemy airspace without detection, but the steep cost of these new aircraft caused considerable criticism. (One was lost during the Gulf War in 1991, and another over Serbia in 1998). The F-117 Nighthawks cost $45 million each, a B-1 Lancer bomber is over $200 million, and each B-2 Spirit exceeds $1 billion. The extraordinary cost of the B-2 has compelled the Air Force to limit itself to less than two dozen of the planes.[69]

The influence of combat-tested fighter pilots on the purchasing policy for fighter aircraft led to a number of changes in the USAF inventory. The General Dynamics F-111 "Aardvark" was a multipurpose tactical fighter-bomber intended to replace the "Century Series" of USAF combat aircraft. It was the first aircraft to have variable-geometry swing-wings. It was also the first to have terrain-following radar (TFR),

---

[69.] Ibid, p. 13.

which automatically guided the aircraft over terrain at altitudes too low for most enemy radar and missiles, although the USAF used the F-111 mainly as a strategic bomber.[70]

The twin-engine McDonnell Douglas F-15 Eagle and the single engine General Dynamics F-16 Fighting Falcon are now the American mainstay fighters in NORAD (alongside the Canadian Forces McDonnell Douglas CF-18 Hornets). Missiles continue to play a major role in the defence of North America. This led to government approval for the development of the LGM 118 Peacekeeper MX missile system, which was capable of carrying 10 Multiple Independently Targetable Warheads (MIRVs). The Minuteman II system carries three.

The MX had enormous destructive power, but was also enormously expensive to build and maintain. There was also a major defense concern in that the MX's were deployed in a relatively small number of silos and would therefore be more vulnerable to a first strike. The fear was that this might be an incentive to launch prematurely, rather than leave the MX silos in a vulnerable position.[71]

---

[70] Edwards Park, *Fighters*, p. 197.
[71] Daniel J. Kaufman, *United States Air Force*, p. 14.

The Gulf War

In the Persian Gulf, the government of Kuwait permitted western agencies to conduct "slant-drilling" operations to remove oil from Iraqi oilfields. The government of Iraq used this as one of its reasons for invading Kuwait in 1990, which had formerly belonged to Iraq. Unfortunately for Iraq, it did not stop its invasion of Kuwait at the border, and Iraqi troops actually marched about six miles into Saudi Arabian territory. The great fear was that in less than six hours, Iraq could have captured the Eastern Province of Saudi Arabia, where most of the Saudi oil reserves are located. Although the Saudis had been asked by the West to cut the Saudi pipelines carrying Iraqi oil to the Gulf, they refused, knowing this would have been considered an act of war. The incursion into Saudi territory, however, caused an immediate request for help to President Bush by Saudi King Faud, and Bush agreed. By the time the request had been actioned, however, the Iraqis had withdrawn back into Kuwait.[72]

One of the perceptions of the threat posed by the invasion was that Iraq could disrupt global petroleum supplies and endanger the independence of many countries in the Middle East. Before the west could fully react, however, Iraq had invaded and then conquered Kuwait.[73]

---

72. Personal observation.
73. William T.Y'Blood, *From the Deserts to the Mountains, Winged Shield, Winged Sword*, p. 441.

The International community was quick to denounce the invasion, with the UN Security Council issuing Resolution 660 to condemn it and demanding Iraq's withdrawal from Kuwait. Iraq ignored the UN's demands. The UN then gave Iraq a deadline of the 15th of January 1991 to leave Kuwait. Meanwhile, within hours of the Iraqi invasion, President Bush ordered two Navy carrier battle groups to deploy to the region. A pair of KC-135 tankers were already in the United Arab Emirates supporting that nation's fighters, and they were ordered to remain in position.[74]

From the 4th of August 1990 preparations were made to force Iraq out of Kuwait. The deployment portion of the war was designated Operation Desert Shield, with the assault phase of the war known as Operation Desert Storm. F-15C Eagle fighters and E-3 Sentry AWACs and KC-10 Contender tankers were among the first USAF dispatched to the region, while soldiers of the 82nd Airborne and the 101st Airborne (Air Assault) Divisions were rapidly airlifted to the area, along with personnel of the 7th Marine Expeditionary Brigade. 99% of the personnel involved in the operation were airlifted in, although sealift was used to carry approximately 85% of the supplies and heavy equipment.[75]

Fully 94% of the Military Airlift Command's C-5 Galaxy (118 of 126), and 74% of its C-141 Starlifter (195 of 265) aircraft took part in the airlift of troops and supplies to the theatre of war. Air Reserve Component units carried their share of the effort, with six Reserve and one Air National Guard C-5 squadrons, ten Reserve and one Guard C-141 squadrons and five C-130 Hercules squadrons from each component taking part. Even these resources were not enough. The Civil Air Reserve Fleet was activated for the first time in its 38-year history which resulted

---

[74] Ibid, p. 447.
[75] Ibid, p. 449.

in the provision of 17 passenger and 21 cargo long-range international aircraft and crews, later supplemented with an additional 76 passenger and 40 cargo aircraft to support the war effort. More airlift support was still required, and therefore Strategic Air Command's KC-10 and KC-135s were also utilized in both airlift and refueling roles.[76]

To run the "air show," General Schwarzkopf assigned the job of Joint Force Air Component Commander to General Horner, the CENTAF commander. Horner became responsible for planning the air campaign and coordinating, allocating and tasking more than 2,700 Coalition aircraft from 14 countries and service components. To ensure that everyone understood Horner's role, General Schwarzkopf stated, "If you aren't part of the air campaign under Horner, you don't fly."[77]

Hours before the assault was launched on Iraq, General Schwarzkopf issued Central Command Operations Order 91-001 stating the Coalition's key objectives:

1. Attack Iraqi political-military leadership and command and control facilities;
2. Gain and maintain air superiority;
3. Sever Iraqi supply lines;
4. Destroy nuclear, biological, and chemical production, storage, and delivery capabilities;
5. Destroy Republican Guard forces;
6. Liberate Kuwait City.[78]

---

[76]. Ibid, p. 449.
[77]. The Coalition nations included Great Britain, France, Canada, and Saudi Arabia who provided combat aircraft and tankers. Ibid, p. 456.
[78]. Ibid, pp. 457-458.

On the evening of the 16th and early on the morning of the 17th of January 1991, the USAF became one of the major instruments used to "sort out" the Iraqi problem in the Persian Gulf War. Coalition aircraft queued up behind some 160 tankers to top off just prior to striking deep into Iraq. Below them, three MH-53J Pave-Low helicopters from the 20th Special Operations Squadron led nine Army AH-64 Apache gunships against Iraqi early-warning radar sites. The radars were quickly destroyed, and this permitted 19 F-15E Eagles to cut through the gap to bomb fixed Scud missile launcher sites in western Iraq. The Eagles were closely followed by three EF-111A Aardvarks, which were assigned to provide electronic counter-measures for a group of 37th Tactical Fighter Wing F-117 Nighthawks who were tasked to strike at the heart of Iraq, the City of Baghdad.[79]

BGM-109C Tomahawk land attack missiles were fired from navy vessels in the Persian Gulf and the Red Sea, and these weapons added to the damage. F-4G Wild Weasel aircraft launched AGM-88 high-speed anti-radiation missiles (HARM) against Iraqi radars, smashing them into oblivion and blinding Iraq's air defense network. Eleven hours after taking off from Barksdale AFB in Louisiana, seven B-52G's from the 2nd Bomb Wing delivered a number of AGM-86C cruise missiles with conventional warheads on targets north of Baghdad. After releasing their missiles, the bombers returned to their base at Barksdale, having conducted a 14,000 mile 35 hour non-stop flight. 10 more B-52Gs from the 379th Bomb Wing would deliver ordnance on Iraq from Wurtsmith AFB, Michigan. 68 "BUFFs" from bases at RAF Fairford, England; Moron, Spain; Diego

---

[79.] Ibid, pp. 458-459.

Garcia, in the Indian Ocean; and several other locations also added the B-52G "hammer" in Desert Storm. Only one B-52 was lost during the war, and this was to an operational accident. It was forced to ditch in the Indian Ocean way back to the island of Diego Garcia, from its bombing mission over Iraq. Eight other B-52s suffered varying degrees of damage from missile and AAA strikes or other causes.[80]

The USAF carried out some 2,759 sorties on the first day of the war alone. USAF transports delivered considerable numbers of combat troops to the battlefield. Fighters, bombers and ground-attack aircraft conducted numerous missions against Iraqi front-line forces, and bombed key targets in Iraq's interior, severely hampering the Iraqi war effort. Spectacular "television" and other media presentations brought the effectiveness of these attacks to the homes of an enthralled western audience. The particularly effective strikes on Iraqi command-and-control centres and communications networks and airfields in Baghdad and other areas of the country were recorded and duly transmitted to the public.[81]

At the start of the war, the Iraqi air forces were equipped with some 700 combat aircraft. These varied in capability, ranging from modern MiG-29 Fulcrum fighters and Su-25 Frogfoot ground-attack aircraft, through MiG-23 Flogger, MiG-25 Foxbat and French F.1 Mirages; to older model MiG-19 Farmer fighters and Tu-16 Badger bombers. These aircraft were theoretically able to operate from some 24 primary airfields and at least 30 dispersal fields. The Iraqi's had an extensive network of hardened aircraft shelters (HAS), but in the end, these proved to be vulnerable to penetrating precision-guided munitions. To protect these aircraft and facilities, the

---

[80.] Ibid, pp. 460-462.
[81.] Daniel J. Kaufman, *United States Air Force*, p. 14.

Iraqis had some 3,679 command-guided missiles of various types, including 7,400 shoulder-fired or road-mobile missiles, 972 anti-aircraft artillery (AAA) sites, 2,404 guns and 6,100 self-propelled AAA guns. This network was laid out in a standard "layered" air defense system. Baghdad's defenses alone included 552 missiles, 380 AAA sites and 1,267 guns, presenting a concentration "thicker than the most heavily defended Warsaw Pact target of the Cold War."[82]

Coalition aircraft hunted relentlessly for the Iraqi air force, sweeping it from the sky in the few occasions where they rose to engage in combat. Although there were a number of modern Iraqi aircraft, the pilots were poorly trained and very rigid in their tactics. They were never very effective, with the Iraqis losing 41 aircraft to coalition forces in the air battles that did take place. Several hundred more were destroyed on the ground. Iraq lost a total of 148 aircraft during the war, including 111 combat aircraft and 37 transports.

The first air-to-air kill of the war was achieved by Captain John K. Kelk of the 33rd Tactical Fighter Wing's 58th Tactical Fighter Squadron. He shot down a MiG-29 Fulcrum, the first of 16 kills for the Tabuk-based F-15C wing. The 36th Tactical Fighter Wing, which flew F-15C Eagles out of Al Kharj and Incirlik, also scored 16 victories. Other units credited with victories include the 1st Tactical Fighter Wing (one Mirage F.1), the 32nd Tactical Fighter Group assigned to the 36th Wing at Incirlik, (one MiG-23 Flogger), the 926th Tactical Fighter Group (one helicopter) and the 10th Tactical Fighter Wing (one Mi-8 Hip helicopter). Two Navy squadrons, VFA-81 (two MiG-21 Fishbeds) and VF-1 (one Mi-8 Hip helicopter),

---

82. William T.Y'Blood, *From the Deserts to the Mountains, Winged Shield, Winged Sword*, p. 444.

received credit for downing Iraqi aircraft, as did the No. 13 Squadron of the Royal Saudi Air Force (two Mirage F.1s). Lieutenant Robert W. Hehemann and Captain Thomas N. Dietz, pilots from the 36th Tactical Fighter Wing, scored three victories apiece.[83]

Coalition fliers learned very quickly that the Iraqi defenses to worry about were their surface-to-air missiles and their AAA fire. Gunfire, missiles and accidents caused the Coalition to lose 75 aircraft, including 33 in combat (27 fixed wing and 5 helicopters). Between the 2nd of August 1990 and the end of the war in 1991, the following Coalition aviation losses were incurred:

US aircraft losses were:
1. 3 out of 84 F-4G/RF-4C Phantom II (USAF)
2. 5 out of 80 A-6E Intruder (USN, USMC)
3. 0 out of 24 EA-6B Prowler (USN)
4. 0 out of 60 A-7 Corsair II (USN, USMC)
5. 6 out of 44 AV-8B Harrier (USMC)
6. 5 out of 96 A-10 Thunderbolt II (USAF) (more than 30 damaged)
7. 1 out of 144 F-14 Tomcat (USN)
8. 4 out of 118 F-15 Eagle C/E (USAF)
9. 11 out of 014 F-16 A/C/E Fighting Falcon (USAF)

---

[83]. Ibid, p. 464.

10. 2 out of 144 F/A-18 Hornet (USN, USMC)
11. 1 out of 50 B-52G Stratofortress (USAF)
12. 0 out of 1 SR-71 Blackbird (USAF)
13. 2 out of 36 F-111/EF-111 Raven (USAF)
14. 1 out of 36 F-117A Nighthawk (USAF)
15. 0 out of 4 U-2R/TR-1A (USAF)
16. 2 out of a number of OV-10 Bronco (USAF)
17. 1 out of a number of AC-130 Spectre Gunship (USAF)
18. 1 out of a number of C-5 Galaxy (USAF)
19. 0 out of 2 E-8A JSTARS (USAF)
20. 3 out of a number of OH-58 Kiowa helicopters
21. 1 out of 185 AH-64 Apache helicopters
22. 3 out of 150 AH-1 Cobra/AH-1W Super Cobra helicopters
23. 6 out of a number of UH-1 Huey helicopters
24. 1 out of a number of CH-47 Chinook helicopters
25. 1 out of a number of CH-46E Sea Knight helicopters
26. 1 out of a number of AH-60/UH-60 Blackhawk helicopters
27. 1 out of a number of SH-60 Sea Hawk helicopters.

UK aircraft losses were

1. 9 out of 66 Tornado
2. 1 out of 16 Jaguar
3. 0 out of 12 Phantom
4. 0 out of 12 Buccaneer
5. 0 out of 21 CH-47 helicopters

6. 0 out of 9 Lynx helicopters
7. 0 out of a number of Sea King helicopters
8. 0 out of 4 Gazelle helicopters
9. 0 out of 15 Puma helicopters
10. Other UK aircraft included the VC-10 Trident, Tristar tankers and Nimrod
    ASW aircraft, for which no losses have been recorded.

French aircraft losses were:
1. 1 out of 23 Mirage F-1CR
2. 0 out of 12 Mirage 2000C
3. 4 damaged out of 27 Jaguar
4. 0 out of 40 Puma helicopters
5. 0 out of a number of Alouette helicopters
6. 0 out of 80 Gazelle helicopters
7. Other French aircraft included C-135 refuelers, C-160G Gabriel and C-130 Hercules, for which no losses have been recorded.

Italian aircraft losses were:
1. 1 out of 10 Tornado

Canada:
1. 0 out of 26 CF-18 Hornet

Saudi Arabia aircraft losses were:
1. 2 out of 44 Tornado
2. 0 out of 58 F-15 Eagle

3. 0 out of 30 Hawk
4. 0 out of 88 F-5 Freedom Fighter
5. 1 out of 45 C-130 Hercules
6. 1 out of 109 Cobra helicopters

Kuwaiti aircraft losses were:
1. 9 out of 24 Mirage F.1
2. 8 out of 27 A-4 Skyhawk
3. 6 out of 6 Hawk
4. 2 out of 23 Gazelle
5. 0 out of 10 Puma
6. 4 out of 4 C-130 Hercules.[84]

Early in the war with the west, Saddam Hussein realized that his airforce could possibly be completely wiped out in a "one-on-one" war of attrition. Taking the long view that he could only keep three of his "political promises," and that he would need to retain as much of his air force as possible intact when the war ended, he chose to keep his aircraft grounded for the most part. He later directed a number of them to fly to Iran to seek sanctuary. Eventually, some 148 Iraqi aircraft including 24 Mirage F.1s, 25 Su-24 Frogfoot and 40 Su-22 Fitter aircraft arrived in Iran, none of which were ever returned to Iraqi hands. Saddam did promise, however, that when the war was over, he would still be in charge of Iraq and that

---

[84.] Personal records from open sources including the "*Stars and Stripes*" newspaper in Germany, 1990-91.

President Bush would be gone; that he would strike Israel again and again, even though no other Muslim nation would; and that he would gather what was left of his forces and put down the Shiite uprising in the south and the Kurdish rebellion in the north. (So far, he has kept all three of his promises, and Iraq still retains 900 fixed and rotary winged aircraft).[85]

The F-117 Nighthawk was used extensively on operations for the first time during the Persian Gulf war, although one was lost exiting the territory of Iraq in an early attack. The media was provided with classic examples of the laser-guided or electro-optically guided "smart bombs" carried by the "stealth" fighter-bomber carrying out "surgical" strikes against key enemy targets. The smart weapons proved to be generally effective, although many of the so-called "iron" bombs were considerable less so. Another critical factor in the mission effectiveness of the allied forces was the use of Air Force satellites, which provided intelligence and communications data, meteorological and navigation data through the system of 24 navigation satellites and ground receivers of the Global Positioning System (GPS). There was also a personnel cost. 26 airmen died during the war.[86]

Aircraft such as the F-15 Eagle on display at Hickam AFB are prime examples of the major "strike" aircraft that were used to carry the attack to Iraq.

Since the Gulf War, the USAF has been involved in a wide variety of missions in the Gulf region. These have included the enforcement of a "no-fly zone" for Iraqi aircraft over extensive areas of Iraq.[87]

---

[85]. Ibid.
[86]. Daniel J. Kaufman, *United States Air Force*, p. 14.
[87]. Ibid, p. 14.

Continuing Service

There are a number of Air Force leaders of the present day USAF who feel that the Air Force of the future will very likely be a close copy of the Air Force of today. They have suggested this will be the likely pattern because of the massive funding that would be required even if they were able to achieve the goals of even a handful of the many research and development projects underway. Limited funding, even judiciously applied, makes it difficult to forge ahead even though the USAF has emphasized the modernization and upgrading of its fleet of aircraft based on continuous research and development. The result is a present day Air Force that employs a "mixed bag" of new equipment which sets the standard of the world while still making effective use of aging modified equipment (the B-52H, for example, is expected to survive another 20 years of service). For these reasons, the replacement of the available forces with large numbers of futuristic systems within the projected available budgets "seems highly unlikely."[88]

Walter Boyne has suggested that the Air Force of the first quarter of the next century will likely be represented by advanced technologies. These would include aircraft such as the Lockheed Martin F-22 Raptor fighter, the McDonnell Douglas C-17A Globemaster III transport, and the Joint Advanced Strike Technology (JAST) fighter. He further suggests that these aircraft are the primary systems that need to be acquired to sustain a modern force. In his opinion,

---

[88]. Walter J. Boyne, *Beyond the Wild Blue, A History of the United States Air Force 1947-1997*, St Martin's Press, New York, 1997, p. 325.

"the Northrop Grumman B-2 Spirit bomber will lead the fleet, but the Rockwell B-1B Lancer, with its greater numbers, much larger payload, and higher speed, will be the primary bomber. The Boeing B-52H Stratofortress will remain in service, as will the Lockheed/Martin F-117A Nighthawk. All strike and bomber aircraft will use precision-guided munitions, including highly refined air launched cruise missiles (ALCMs). Refueling support will be provided by the existing tanker fleet, possibly supplemented by some tankers modified from civilian airliners.[89]

Boyne estimates that the F-22 Raptor procurement "will extend to about 450 aircraft. The number of JAST fighters is undetermined." There may only be 21 B-2 Spirit bombers procured, and "there are currently (only) 84 B-1 Lancers and 85 B-52Hs in active service."[90]

Boyne's conclusion as to the future of the USAF is that despite the realities of budgetary limitations and the myriad, formless threats that lie ahead, there is one undying constant that will never change, and that guarantees the success of the Air Force in the future and ensures that it will remain the mainstay of U.S. national defense. That constant is the quality and dedication of the personnel who volunteer to serve in its ranks, to accept the difficulties of service life, and to excel in meeting whatever challenges the future presents. No matter what lies ahead, the people of the United States Air Force will continue to do the planning, improvising, sacrificing, fighting, and the dying, necessary (to keep the United States free).[91]

---

[89] Ibid, p. 326.
[90] Ibid, p. 326.
[91] Ibid, p. 328.

Statement of the Secretary of Defense on the War on Terrorism

The War on terrorism is on everyone's minds as this book goes to press. Each of us has a point of view on where it will lead. While on duty in NORAD, our commander passed us this statement which was released by Secretary of Defense Donald H. Rumsfeld on the 1st of November 2001. I believe his statement says exactly what needed to be said.

Good afternoon.

I have reflected on some of the questions posed at the last briefing: questions about the 'speed of progress' in the campaign-questions about the "patience" of the American people-if something does not happen immediately. I have a sense that the public understands the following facts:

On September 11th terrorists attacked New York and Washington, DC, murdering thousands of innocent people–Americans and people from dozens of countries and all races and religions–in cold blood. On October 7th, less than a month later, we had positioned coalition forces in the region, and we began military operations against Taliban and Al-Qa'ida targets throughout Afghanistan. Since that time, roughly three weeks ago, coalition forces have flown over 2,000 sorties, broadcast 300-plus hours of radio transmissions, delivered an amazing 1,030,000 humanitarian rations to starving Afghan people.

Today is November 1, and smoke, at this very moment, is still rising from the ruins of the World Trade Center. With the ruins still smoldering and the smoke not yet cleared, it seems to me that Americans understand well that, despite the urgency in the press questions, we are still in the very, very early stages of this war. The ruins are still smoking!

Consider some historical perspective:

After the December 1941 attack on Pearl Harbor, it took four months before the United States responded to that attack with the Doolittle raid of April 1942.

It took eight months after Pearl Harbor before the U.S. began a land campaign against the Japanese, with the invasion of Guadalcanal in August of 1942.

The U.S. bombed Japan for three-and-a-half years, until August 1945, before we accomplished our objectives in the Pacific.

On the European front, the allies bombed Germany continually for nearly five years, from September of 1940 until May of 1945.

It took 11 months to start the land campaign against the Germans, with the invasion of North Africa in November of 1942.

It took the United States two years and six months after Hitler declared war on us before we landed in France on June 6, 1944.

We are now fighting a new kind of war. It is unlike any America has ever fought before. Many things about this war are different from wars past-but, as I have said, one of those differences is not the possibility of instant victory. At my briefing when I announced the start of the air campaign on October 7th, I stated that our initial goals were:

To make clear to the Taliban that harboring terrorists carries a price;

To acquire intelligence to facilitate future operations against Al-Qa'ida and the Taliban;

To develop useful relationships with groups in Afghanistan that oppose the Taliban and Al-Qa'ida; to make it increasingly difficult for the terrorists to use Afghanistan freely as a base of operation;

To alter the military balance over time by denying to the Taliban the offensive systems that hamper the progress of the various opposition forces; and,

To provide humanitarian relief to Afghans suffering oppressive living conditions under the Taliban regime.

That was 24 days ago, three weeks and three days, not three months or three years, but three weeks and three days. We have made measurable progress on each of these goals. The attacks of September 11 were not days or weeks but years in the making. The terrorists were painstaking and deliberate, and it appears they may have spent years planning their activities. There is no doubt in my mind but that the American people know that it's going to take more than 24 days.

I also stated that our task is much broader than simply defeating the Taliban or Al-Qa'ida, it is to root out global terrorist networks, not just in Afghanistan, but wherever they are, to ensure that they cannot threaten the American people or our way of life. This is a task that will take time to accomplish. Victory will require that every element of American influence and power be engaged.

Americans have seen tougher adversaries than this before-and they have had the staying power to defeat them. Underestimating the American people is a bad bet. In the end, war is not about statistics, deadlines, short attention spans, or 24-hour news cycles. It is about will, the projection of will, the clear, unambiguous determination of the President and the American people to see this through to certain victory.

In other American wars, enemy commanders have come to doubt the wisdom of taking on the strength and power of this nation and the resolve of her people. I expect that somewhere, in a cave in Afghanistan, there is a terrorist leader who is, at this moment, considering precisely the same thing.

For all those who fly for, and serve in the defense of North America, particularly since the terrorist attack on the World Trade Center and the Pentagon on 11 September and in the ongoing war against terrorism, we thank you. The aim of this book was to record and identify the locations of where at least some those aircraft which have been used in that defense can be found in Alaska. They are, in fact, Alaska Warbird Survivors.

There is a far better way to protect our homes and our people than to fight and win a great war. The better way is to be so obviously superior in our ability to carry the war to an enemy that he will not take the risk of starting one.
Chief of Staff General Thomas D. White.

Japanese Aircraft That Participated in Attacks on Alaska

There are two Japanese aircraft that have direct WWII connections with Alaska, although few exist today, the Mitsubishi A6M2 Zero fighter, and the Aichi D3A Val dive-bomber.

Mitsubishi A6M2 Zero fighter

The Mitsubishi A6M Zero-Sen or type 0 fighter was a fast, nimble, single-seat, long-range interceptor-fighter airplane powered by one 1,130hp Nakajima Sakae 31 radial piston engine. It had a maximum speed of 346 mph, a service ceiling of 35,000', and a maximum range of 1,118 miles. The A6M2 was armed with two 20mm cannon in the wings and three 13.2mm machine-guns (two in the wings and one in the nose). Designed by Jiro Horikoshi, the Zero had the ability to turn more tightly than any allied aircraft. American pilots in the early stages of the war learned that they had to avoid dog-fights with the Zero and instead use their greater diving speed and overwhelming firepower to defeat it. The Zero was vulnerable, however, because it obtained its range and quickness by sacrificing armor, structural strength, and self-sealing fuel tanks. It did not take many hits to knock it down.[92]

As the Japanese invasion of China moved farther inland, a need arose for a fighter with a much longer range to escort bombers to and from their

---

[92.] bid, p. 214.

targets. It was this requirement for a combination of speed, range and maneuverability that led to the development of the Japanese A6M fighter. Designed to 1937 specifications and first flown on 1 April 1939, the A6M was ordered into series production as the Navy's type "0" carrier fighter and thus the basis for the name "Zero". The allied designation was "Zeke". In July 1940 A6M-2s appeared in the skies over China. While only 328 A6M-2s were in operation at the beginning of World War II, 11,283 were ultimately produced by war's end.

Credited with mystical powers of maneuverability, what made the Zero a great combat aircraft during the early stages of World War II was the high level of experience of Japanese pilots. In all other respects the A6M was rapidly out classed by newer allied fighters. The lack of self-sealing fuel tanks and armor protection for the pilot as well as a tendency for the controls to stiffen at high speeds, made the A6M extremely vulnerable to attack.

Still, opposition fighter pilots made it a point to avoid a one-on-one confrontation, the escape from which was a steep dive. Converting altitude advantage to speed for a slashing attack and recovery coupled with other tactics such as the Thach Weave led to the high kill ratios achieved by the F4F Wildcat during the early years of WW II.

There is an excellent example of a Zero on display in the NMNA. The Museum's aircraft is an A6M-2B Model 21 (Serial No. 5450), and it was recovered from an abandoned fighter strip on Ballele Island near Bougainville and partially restored by Black Shadow Aviation of Jacksonville, Florida. *Information courtesy of the National Museum of Naval Aviation.*

The first Japanese Zero captured intact was found on Akutan Island. Its pilot died after a forced landing following a Japanese attack with Zeros and Vals on Dutch Harbor on the 3rd and 4th of June 1942. This attack had been conducted by 16 fighter and torpedo bombers flying from the Imperial Japanese Navy (IJN) aircraft carrier Ryujo. The Zero's wreckage was found inverted with the pilots body five weeks later. An evaluation and recovery team quickly shipped the aircraft back to the continental US for study.[93]

Aichi D3A Val

The Val was a two-seat carrier or land-based dive-bomber powered by one 1,070-hp Mitsubishi Kinsei 44 radial piston engine. It had a maximum speed of 239 mph, a service ceiling of 30,510' and a range of 913 miles. It was armed with two 7.7mm fixed forward-firing Type 97 machine guns and one 7.7 mm Type 92 machine-gun on a flexible gunmount in the rear cockpit. The Val carried one 551 lb and two 132 lb bombs. The Val was designed as a low-wing monoplane with fixed landing gear. It began production in December 1939 under the designation Navy Type 99 Carrier Bomber Model 11 (Aichi D3A1). A total of 129 Vals participated in the attack on Pearl Harbor. A Japanese task force of Vals also later sank the British aircraft carrier HMS Hermes and the cruisers HMS Cornwall and HMS Dorsetshire in April 1942.[94] Vals remained in service to the end of the war, and many were used for training and in the Kamikaze role. *Information courtesy of the National Museum of Naval Aviation.*

[93.] John Hale Cloe, *The Aleutian Warriors, A History of the 11th Air Force and Fleet Air Wing 4, Part 1*, Anchorage Chapter, Air Force Association and Pictorial History, Missoula, Montana, 1990, p. 134 and p. 175.

[94.] James J. Haggerty and Warren Reiland Smith, *The U.S. Air Force*, p. 76.

APPENDIX A

A short list of Alaska Warbirds

Kulis ANG Base Museum

Douglas C-47A Skytrain (Serial No. 0315497) (42-100857)
Fairchild C-123J Provider (Serial No. 56-4395)
Lockheed P-80 Shooting Star (Serial No. 91849)
Lockheed T-33A Shooting Star (Serial No. 35403)
North American T-6G Texan (Serial No. 453015A), painted as 34555 (This aircraft was the first Texan in the Alaska ANG)
North American F-86A Sabre (Serial No. 12807) (49-1195)

Eielson AFB

Cessna O-2A Skymaster (Serial No. 68-11003)
Fairchild A-10 Thunderbolt II (Serial No. 75-0289)
General Dynamics F-16A Fighting Falcon (Serial No. 78-0052)
McDonnell F-4C Phantom II (Serial No. 64-0905)
Lockheed T-33 Shooting Star (Serial No. 53-6064), under restoration

Elmendorf AFB

Convair F-102A Delta Dagger (Serial No.61274) (56-1053)
Lockheed P-38G Lightning (Serial No. 42-13400)

Lockheed T-33A Shooting Star (Serial No. 36021)
McDonnell F-4C Phantom II (Serial No. 66-723)
McDonnell F-4C Phantom II (Serial No. 64-0890)
McDonnell Douglas F-15A Eagle (Serial No. 94081)
Northrop F-89J Scorpion (Serial No. 32453)
Piasecki CH-21 Shawnee helicopter (Serial No. 52-8696)

Alaska Aviation Heritage Museum, Anchorage

American Pilgrim 100B (Serial No.)
AT-19 (Serial No.)
Beechcraft UC-45F Expeditor (Serial No.)
Bell UH-1H Iroquois "Huey" (Serial No.)
Bellanca Pacemaker CH-300 (Serial No.)
Bellanca Sr. Pacemaker (fuselage) (Serial No.)
Cessna T-50 Bushmaster (Serial No.)
Consolidated PBY-5A Catalina Canso (wreck) (Serial No.)
Curtiss Robin (Serial No.)
Douglas DWC World Cruiser "Seattle" (Serial No.)
Fairchild 24G (Serial No.)
Fairchild FC2W2 (frame) (Serial No.)
Ford 5-AT Trimotor (wreck) (Serial No.)
Grumman Goose G-21A (Serial No.)
Grumman G-44 Widgeon (Serial No.)
Grumman J2F-6 Duck (Serial No.)
Hamilton Metalplane H47 (Serial No.)
Keystone Loening K1-84 (Serial No.)
Noordyn C-64A Norseman Mk. IV (Serial No.)
S-43 (nose only) (Serial No.)
Spartan Executive (Serial No.)
Spencer Aircar (Serial No.)
Stearman C2B (Serial No.)

Stinson AT-19 Reliant (Serial No.)
Stinson L-5 Sentinel (Serial No.)
Stinson SR Jr. (Serial No.)
Stinson SR-9 Gullwing CM (Serial No.)
Stinson 108 (Serial No.)
Travel Air 6000B (float) (Serial No.)
Waco UIC (Serial No.)
Waco YKC (float) (Serial No.)

Alaskaland Pioneer Air Museum, Fairbanks

Baking Duce II (F.M. 1) (Serial No.)
Beech UC-45F (Serial No.)
Bell UH-1H Iroquois "Huey" helicopter (Serial No.)
Fairchild 24J (Serial No.)
Fokker Super Universal (frame) (Serial No.)
Martyn B-10 Bomber (Serial No.)
MX Quicksilver (Serial No.)
Noordyn C-64A Norseman Mk. IV (Serial No.)
Pereira S.P. 3 (Serial No.)
Raven S-50 (Serial No.)
Rotorway 133 (Serial No.)
Rutan Vari-EZ (Serial No.)
Ryan PT-22 (ST3KR) (Serial No.)
Sikorsky HO4S Chickasaw helicopter
Stinson SR-5 Jr. (Serial No.)
Vultee V-77/AT-19 Reliant (Serial No.)
Healy, Denali Wings
Ford Tri-Motor (Serial No.)
Kenair, City static display
Lockheed T-33A Shooting Star (Serial No. 52-9772)

Wasilla, Museum of Alaska Transportation & Industry

Bell UH-1H Iroquois "Huey" (Serial No.)
Bowers 1-A Flybaby (homebuilt)
Cessna T-50 Bobcat (Serial No.)
Clerget 50 hp 4-cylinder in-line engine (1912)
Convair F-102A Delta Dagger (Serial No. 56-1282)
Cunningham-Hall PT-6 (1929)
Curtis Challenger 6-cylinder radial engine
Douglas C-47 Skytrain (Serial No. 42-100857)
Douglas C-47A Skytrain (Serial No. 43-15200)
Cunningham-Hall PT-6 (1929)
Fairchild 71 (1929)
Fairchild C-123J Provider (Serial No.)
Fike "E" (homebuilt)
Franklin 65 hp engine
German V-1 "Buzz Bomb" replica, (manufactured by the Ford Motor Co. for testing)
Jacobs radial engine
Lawrence A-3 2-cylinder opposed engine
Lockheed Electra 10A (Serial No.)
Lycoming "300" radial engine
Lycoming "Open Rocket" radial engine
Lycoming D-145 engine
Menasco "Super Pirate" 4-cylinder inverted engine
Mitchell B-10 Flying Wing (ultra-light)
OX-5 engine
Piasecki H-21B Shawnee helicopter (Serial No. 53-4362)
Pratt & Whitney 28-cylinder "Corncob" radial engine
Pratt & Whitney 985 radial engine
Rand KR-1 (homebuilt)
Ranger 6-cylinder inverted engine

Rotec Panther (ultra-light)
Sikorsky H-5H Dragonfly helicopter (Serial No.)

BIBLIOGRAPHY

Air Force Pamphlet 36-2241, Volume 1, 01 July 1999, Personnel, Promotion Fitness Examination (PFE) Study Guide, Chapter 3, Air Force History.

BOYNE, Walter J. *Beyond the Wild Blue, A History of the United States Air Force 1947-1997.* New York, St Martin's Press, 1997.

CRAGG, Dan. *Guide to Military Installations, 4th Edition.* Mechanicsburg, PA, Stackpole Books, 1994.

CRAVEN, Wesley F., and CATE, James L. *The Army Air Forces in World War II, Vol. I: Plans and Early Operations, January 1939 to August 1942; Vol. II: Europe: Torch to Pointblank, August 1942 to December 1943; Vol. III: Europe: Argument to V-E Day, January 1944 to May 1945; Vol. IV: The Pacific: Guadalcanal to Saipan, August 1942 to July 1944; Vol. V: The Pacific: Matterhorn to Nagasaki, June 1944 to August 1945; Vol VI: Men and Planes; Vol. VII: Services Around the World.* (University of Chicago Press, 1948-1958). Reprinted for the Air Force History and Museums Program, 1983.

CLOE, John Hale. *The Aleutian Warriors, A History of the 11th Air Force and Fleet Air Wing 4, Part 1.* Missoula, Montana, Anchorage Chapter, Air Force Association and Pictorial History, 1990.

COHEN, Stan. *The Forgotten War, Vol. 1, A Pictorial History of WWII in Alaska and North Western Canada*. Missoula, Montana, Pictorial Histories Publishing Company, Inc, 1981.

DONALD, David, General Editor. *The Complete Encyclopedia of World Aircraft. The development and specifications of over 2500 civil and military aircraft from 1903 to the present day*. New York, Barnes & Noble Books, 1999.

EVINGER, William R. Editor, *Directory of US Military Bases Worldwide, Third Edition*, Oryx Press, 1998.

FREEMAN, Roger A. *The Mighty Eighth, Units, Men and Machines (A History of the US 8th Army Air Force)*. New York, Doubleday and Company, Inc., Garden City, 1970.

FUTRELL, Robert F. *The United States Air Force in Korea, 1950-1953*. Duell, Sloan and Pearce, revised 1983, 1991.

HAGGERTY, James J. and Smith, Warren Reiland. *The U.S. Air Force: A Pictorial History in Art*. New York, Books, Inc., Publishers, 1966.

HALLION, Richard P. *Storm Over Iraq, Air power and the Gulf War*. Air Force Historian, 1992.

KAUFMAN, Daniel J., B.Sc., M.P.A., Ph.D. *Understanding International Relations* and *U.S. National Security Strategy for the 1990s*.

MAURER, Maurer, (General Editor). *The U.S. Air Service in World War 1. Vol. I: The Final Report of the Chief of Air Service AEF and a tactical History; Vol. II: Early Concepts of Military Aviation; Vol. III: The Battle of St.*

Mihel; Vol. IV: Postwar Review. Air Force History and Museums Program, 1978, 1979.

NALTY, Bernard C. *Winged Shield, Winged Sword, A History of the United States Air Force*, Air Force History and Museums Program, USAF, Washington, D.C. 1997.

PARK, Edwards. *Fighters, The World's Great Aces and Their Planes*. New York, Barnes & Noble Books, 1990.

SALISBURY, C.A. *Soldiers of the Mists, Minutemen of the Alaska Frontier*. Missoula, Montana, Pictorial Histories Publishing Company, Inc., 1992.

UBBELOHDE, Carl, BENSON, Maxine Benson and SMITH, Duane A. *Alaska History, Seventh Edition*. Boulder, Alaska, Pruett Publishing Company, 1999.

ABOUT THE AUTHOR

Harold A. Skaarup

Major Hal Skaarup is an Army officer presently serving in the Intelligence Branch of the Canadian Forces (CF). Hal joined the Canadian Militia while attending the College of Trades and Technology in St. John's, Newfoundland in 1971. He later became an officer through the Reserve Officer University Training Program (ROUTP), and after completing his training at Shilo, Manitoba, was commissioned in 1973. In 1974 he completed his Bachelor of Fine Arts (BFA) degree, graduating from the Nova Scotia College of Art and Design (NSCAD) in Halifax. Between 1977 and 1981 he was a member of the Canadian Forces Parachute Team, the "Skyhawks," participating in airshows across Canada and parts of United States. He is still an active skydiver with more than 1700 jumps to date.

As a reserve intelligence officer, Hal served a two-year tour of duty in the Headquarters, Canadian Forces in Europe (CFE) in Lahr, Germany from 1979 to 1983. In the summer of 1983, he transferred to the Regular Force and he was then sent to the Canadian Forces School of Intelligence and Security (CFSIS), first as a student, and later as an instructor. Between 1984 and 1986 he served as an intelligence analyst in Ottawa and then from 1986 to 1989 as the Regimental Intelligence Officer (R Int O) for the Canadian Airborne Regiment (CAR). As a Captain in the CAR, Hal went to the island of Cyprus on United Nation's (UN) duty from 1986-87. (In 1988, all those who had worn the "Blue Beret" on peacekeeping duty were awarded the Nobel Peace Prize.) The following year he completed the Canadian Forces Staff School (CFSS) course in

Toronto. One year later he also completed the six month Canadian Land Forces Command and Staff Course (CLFCSC, also known as Fox Hole U), in Kingston, Ontario.

On completing CLFCSC in 1989, Hal was again posted to Lahr, Germany where he served as the Intelligence officer for the 4th Canadian Mechanized Brigade Group (4 CMBG), with the First Canadian Division (Forward). This came at one of the most interesting periods of change in modern European history. In 1992, he was posted back to CFSIS. On promotion to Major in 1993, he became the Officer Commanding (OC) the Intelligence Training Company, and later the Distance Learning Company at CFSIS. In 1994, Major Skaarup was posted to CFB Gagetown, News Brunswick, as the Intelligence Directing Staff (Int DS) officer in the Tactics School (Tac Sch) at the Combat Training Centre (CTC), where he was also "dual hatted" as the Base G2. Between instructing on and participating in numerous field exercises as the commander of the "Enemy Forces," he completed his Master of Arts Degree in War Studies through the Royal Military College (RMC), receiving his degree on graduation in May 1997 at Kingston, Ontario. In June 1997, he was posted to Sarajevo on a six month tour of duty as the Commanding Officer (CO) of the Canadian National Intelligence Centre (CANIC) in support of the Canadian Contingent of the NATO led Peace Stabilization Force (CC SFOR) in Bosnia-Herzegovina.

In June 1999, Major Skaarup completed the year long Land Forces Technical Staff Course (LFTSC) with RMC's Department of Applied Military Science (AMS) in Kingston. He is presently posted to Colorado where he is the Chief of the North American Aerospace Defence Command (NORAD) Exercise Intelligence Section, J2SZ in Cheyenne Mountain in Colorado Springs. If you have questions or comments on the aircraft mentioned in the "Warbird Survivors" series, his e-mail address is *h.skaarup@worldnet.att.net.*

0-595-20918-1